1988

MEANINGFUL COUNSELING

MEANINGFUL COUNSELING
A Guide for Students, Counselors, and Clergy

Marian D. Robinson, Ph.D.

University of Portland
Portland, Oregon

 **HUMAN SCIENCES PRESS, INC.**
72 FIFTH AVENUE
NEW YORK, N.Y. 10011

Printed in the United States of America
0 987654321

Library of Congress Cataloging-in-Publication Data

Robinson, Marian D.
  Meaningful counseling.

  Bibliography: p.
  Includes index.
  1. Counseling. 2. Personality. I. Title.
[DNLM: 1. Counseling. 2. Personality. WM 55 R663m]
BF637.C6R58   1988   158'.3   87-3213
ISBN 0-89885-385-0

CONTENTS

5

ACKNOWLEDGMENTS

Special thanks is due to the following publishers for permission to quote from various texts: Yale University Press; Review of Existential Psychology and Psychiatry; Charles Scribner's Sons: Alfred A. Knopf, Inc.; and Citadel Press. Selections from *Existentialism and Human Emotions* by Jean Paul Sartre reprinted with permission of The Philosophical Library, New York, NY (1957). Selections from *Existential Psychology* by Rollo May reprinted with permission of Random House, Inc. (1961). Selections from *Fallible Man, Part II, Finitude and Guilt* by Paul Ricoeur reprinted by permission of Fordham University Press (1965). Selections from *Personalism* by Emmanuel Mounier reprinted by permission of Routledge & Kegan Paul, Ltd., London, England (1952).

Every book is the result of many positive contributions and supports. The assistance, enthusiasms, and help of many generous individuals form an important part of the end product.

I am deeply grateful to all the Robinsons, especially James and Mathilda, Leo, Dolores, Jim, Francis, and Alphonse, for their ongoing support and encouragement of my writing endeavors. I owe special thanks to the Western Humanities Foundation for supporting the beginnings of this research. Likewise, I want to thank the University of Portland Faculty Research Grants Committees for providing several summers of research opportunities, and the Department of Psychology and Social Sciences for ongoing encouragement and assistance. Special thanks is also due to the patience and perseverance of the University of Portland's secretarial personnel, especially Mary Ward and Norma Snyder.

I owe a special debt of gratitude to Professor Paul Ricoeur of the Sorbonne, Paris, for reading the first draft and offering helpful suggestions, and also to Dr. Bernadette Carlson, S.N.J.M. for her helpful review of the manuscript. I want to thank Dr. Raymond J. Steimel of the Catholic University of America for providing many years of participation and professional experiences in the Counseling Workshops. I also want to thank many of my colleagues and alumni of Marylhurst College for their continued enthusiasm and helpful assistance.

Above all, I am deeply grateful to Norma Fox, Editor-in-Chief of Human Sciences Press for her invaluable insights and wise counsel.

Marian D. Robinson S.N.J.M.

PREFACE

The purpose of this book is to provide students, counselors, pastoral advisors, religious directors, parents, and all others whose responsibilities include the helping arts, with a humanistic guide to counseling. This work is the outcome of many influences and experiences. Dr. Carl Rogers, as a professor of counseling, provided an awareness of the humanistic dimension. Dr. Sabert Basescu, a professor of existential psychology, opened vast unknown horizons of thought. The opportunity to participate in international seminars and phenomenology under Professor Van Breda of Louvain University, Belgium, provided unusual insights into the works of Husserl and his phenomenological psychology. Above all, with the help of my good friend, the French philosopher, Gabriel Marcel, the meaning of existential thought as applied to human relationships was clarified. Marcel himself was an examplar of warmth and caring and of willingness to share his own genius. All of these expositions of existential thought, personality development, and humanistic counseling share deep common bonds and goals, namely the meaning and achievement of a positive integrated human person.

In effective counseling one has to know the nature of personality, the chronological stages through which it evolves, and how it matures in the becoming process. It is equally important to understand the mental defenses and experiences that may contribute to the disintegration of personality. The anxieties, depressions, withdrawals, and the tensions that the client here and now experiences create the pain and suffering in his illness.

It is the ability of the counselor to provide a meaningful encounter, as well as his knowledge of causes, which will bring relief to the client. In order to accomplish all this, the counselor must also know well the developmental phases of communication beginning with infancy and continuing to adulthood and beyond.

It is hoped that the readers of this guide will experience a newness of being in their own lives and become aware of their own potentials and means of self-actualization and also be able to help their clients attain the same achievements.

Chapter 1

INTRODUCTION

Goals of Counseling

The counseling process is a helping relationship and is directed toward assisting the client in experiencing a lessening of mental tension and in achieving a sense of well-being. Counseling involves interpersonal exchanges between a trained counselor and a person who seeks relief from mental anguish, indecision, or perhaps painful inadequacies. The diversity of counseling areas spans a wide range of mental problems and includes a variety of counseling experts, depending upon the needs of the client. Clinicians, pastoral counselors, social workers, personnel directors, and many others are expected to fulfill some measure of counseling in their work. Depending upon training and skill, the counselor usually works with individuals whose needs he can best serve. But all counselors, regardless of their focus, require a comprehensive and in-depth knowledge of personality and motivation in order to be effective helpers.

Mental pain arises from some lack of harmony within the personality. Just as the health of the body depends upon the smooth interaction of the physiological systems, so does mental health depend upon the integration of personality dynamics. In order to help and to heal, the counselor needs to know the developmental stages of personality. Deeper than personality is the client's motivational system. Herein lies the key to successful counseling. To understand a client, to be of help to him, the counselor must be able to comprehend his inner reality, namely, his personality organization and his motivational patterns.

Counseling is also a learning process. The client needs to become aware of certain mental habits that are barriers to his freedom. Through counseling he learns to free himself of these impediments and then to replace these old habits with new growth-producing activities. The counselor provides the setting for the movements of change. He facilitates the learning experience by his presence, his sensitivity, his listening attitudes, and his ability to assist the client in pursuing his own self-knowledge.

The authentic counselor knows well the sequence of developmental stages and is able to identify inmature residuals in the grown person. When he works with children or adolescents, likewise he is able to recognize behavioral patterns that are typical of each developmental stage, and know whether or not this child's level is mature for his age. It is the keen awareness of these underlying principles that enables the counselor to be at ease with himself in order to be a skillful helper.

Chapter 2

PERSONALITY AND MOTIVATION

Personality is a movement of the whole person in his relatedness to everyone and everything outside of himself. It is the person expressing himself to others, putting his ideas into action, being a person-in-the-world. The being-ness of a man means being with and for others. This is the human person in his full capacity. Insofar as his being-ness for others is limited, so is he limited in his personality. As a person, ontologically, he always remains whole and entire, continual in his existence, subject in his own inalienable dignity, and essentially this individual. But in his personality, i.e., in his self-extension, the person exists in, and must move along in, the flow of reality. His own subjectivity is continually in flux as ideas, images, and feelings pass in quick succession through his consciousness. A simple exercise in recall demonstrates the limitations of reflection in trying to recapture even for a day or a few hours all his subjective data.

If we attempt at the day's end to enumerate all of the images or ideas of which we were aware during the previous hours we realize that a complete recollection is impossible. They have not evaporated, but have been assimilated into the flux as it continues endlessly on its course. Subjectivity is not composed of a series of elements, or contents that become points on a line; it is, of its nature, a flow of internalizations, some of greater intensity than others. In the objective world surrounding us, everything that is living is also in observable movement, and even within inanimate beings change occurs, though perhaps less perceptibly. This is the nature of subjective and objective reality—movement, flux, and evolution. What remains unchanged is the being-ness or existence in reality and all that it includes. Whatever exists and is, cannot not exist, or not be, in the total sense. The fact remains that even for objects destroyed, potential existence remains.

What we want to grasp here is that the person in his fullest reality must increase in his extension as he continues to exist and to be. He cannot remain stationary even if he would choose to do so. The human person through his personality grows and becomes, and his personality matures as he discriminates and assimilates through his choices. The effectiveness of his personality, then, depends on his own self-direction. He must constantly perceive, evaluate, and choose what he assimilates in his self-becoming. His choices bring together the divergent forms of knowing and feeling and unite them into his individualized expressions. His expressions will depend on particular physiological structures and bodily characteristics, but they will also transcend his physical properties. The effectiveness of his personality, his maturity of personal relationships, will depend not on his physical strength, but on his ego strength. It is in the subjective world of self, then, that we find the sources of effective or ineffective personality.

AUTHENTIC PERSONALITY

The mature personality is attained from positive growth over a long period of time. In its maturity it is always pliant, continuing in its becoming. Maturity in personality is not a certain level that is reached and held permanently. The very essence of a mature personality is its capacity to change and continue in its positive growth. Personality changes also occur in the deterioration of psychotics and neurotics, but these changes are destructive. Positive changes are constructive and expansive. Maturity means flexibility and the power to direct energies in different modes, different intensities, and different directions. It is the power to proportion and to regulate effectively the dynamic flow within to the situation without. It is the capacity to be open to others without decisive effort, to be sufficiently free from self-engrossment as to be ready to receive another, to be pliant in adjusting internally to the subjective needs of another. This facility of self-direction requires a mature self, confident in its ego strength, full in a sense of beingness, ready to be present to another.

The sources of personality formation combine environmental influences and internalized meanings. It is the self which unites the outer world with the inner subjectivity; it is the self who receives the environment and, in turn, transforms it into modes of self-expression. The particular way in which experiences are integrated will be influenced by levels of growth. Within the subjectivity of each person there are two distinct modes, knowledge and action, and in each of these modes a variety of functions formulate knowing and doing.

Maturity is an intricate network of felt evaluations. To become a strong motive, something must be known, and also dynamically embraced. What is known is not always dynamically sought. The wide differences in human performances are explained by numerous factors but the most crucial ones will be understood in terms of motivation. Self-directed activities are motivated; some inner synthesis has joined knowing and choosing, and self-directed behavior is the result. Many acts of knowledge are followed by dynamic activity but not exteriorly executed. For example, a man may read an account of the achievements of two different athletes and decide which one is better, but he may never express his decision. Self-directional behavior becomes the outward manifestation of knowledge, evaluated, dynamically accepted, and outwardly expressed.

MOTIVATIONAL SYSTEMS

In the motivation process, ideas are compared and judged and in the light of these intellectual analyses, some are discarded, others inhibited or suppressed, and others selected and pursued. These become the most influential measures in the life of a human person. On these thresholds decisions are made; some may influence the whole life cycle of this person and his associates; others may be of small consequence. These intimate circles disclose the dispositions and responses that will form the personality. The feeling element is very strong here and can significantly change the real knowing. Psychology has much research to explain the nature of knowing, but a meager amount to help us grasp how the dynamic energies, on some levels, change this knowledge and, on other levels, direct the acceptance of it. The unconscious factors in our feelings contribute strongly to the final outcome. The stronger the unconscious factors in an individual, the less able he is to regulate his personality development. In the case of neurotics and psychotics the unconscious influences are so strong that self-direction is minimal, and the personality formation warps or disintegrates.

Motivation is also a growth process and passes through many stages proportional to the general increase of the individual. Motivation as a power to stimulate action must be known intellectually and appreciated dynamically. This ability is the crucial aspect in effective motivation. If a parent, a teacher, or a manager wishes to provide motivation for others, he must do so within the intellectual range and the dynamic scope of the individuals concerned. Age groups, economic levels, etc., share common bonds and have general interests and potentials. But the experiences of individuals, causing unique differences, render motivation for long-range purposes a personal enterprise. What a person in his inner sanctum holds as his aspirations will be the key to motivation for him.

GENERALIZED GOALS

Generalized goals are similar for most: Health, happiness, work satisfaction, and freedom from stress influence our habits. But what an individual sees as achievement for himself, or as happiness, will include specific aspects related to himself alone. More important, motivation for a particular individual means an appeal for action related to his uniqueness. He acts in a certain manner because it holds meaning for him, whether understood by another or not. (There is no stereotyped pattern of behavior and no stereotyped set of motives.) An action may be performed for itself if it holds meaning for the individual. There may not be any outside purpose, but merely the action itself that appeals to him. A man may find satisfaction in working a puzzle not because he hopes to sharpen his wits or to pass the time, but simply because he likes to manipulate the rings. He may walk for the sake of walking. Most activities have more definite goals, but are always related to an individual's appraisal, no matter how the rest of the world evaluates the same thing.

Generalized motives attract most persons, but individual personality and behavior result from motives tied in with a person's own image of self-esteem and whatever he sees and feels to be helpful to his own fulfillment. His subjective world of ideas and feelings is the mold for motivations. The more I know about another's subjective world, the more effectively I can motivate him, and vice versa. If an adolescent derives greatest satisfaction from athletics, then he will be motivated toward generosity more through games than through books. If a man's image of himself as a successful person is that of a man of wealth, then whatever brings him money will motivate his behavior. If a man's self-image equates his success with knowledge, then he will be motivated to acquire learning. His positive image of self-esteem is the result of parental affection experienced during his period of development. The ideas children and adolescents have realized in love and joy will be the ones they seek to fulfill later as adults. Whatever experiences of pain, hate, or fear they associate with the behavior of adults or others will be the ones they avoid consciously or unconsciously as they mature. A man may be easily motivated to courageous acts because as a child he grew up in an atmosphere of love and witnessed demonstrations of courage. A person who is motivated most strongly by fear, or who fearfully seeks to avoid many activities—driving a car, swimming, assuming responsibility—grows up in an environment of fear and dread. Motivating him by threats will be effective but will arouse resentment. Whatever means freedom from tension for him will be the strongest motivation of all. Competition will not appeal to the fearful because it increases tension. For the courageous person, competition may, despite the tension, tie in with his ideas of challenge, overbalancing the fear of tension, and become a strong motivation.

MOTIVATION AND PERSONAL GROWTH

Motivation is closely allied to personality growth because it will depend on the individual's felt-knowledge in relating to others. If childhood or adolescence has been spent in an environment with a pragmatic orientation, then the person will seek to relate to others on that basis. If, on the contrary, he witnessed the joyful effects of having parents who mutually loved one another, who enjoyed encounter, his motivation to relate generously to others will be facilitated. However, motivation can be developed contrary to such experiences. But in the beginning of motivation development, the strongest influences will come from sources perceived and felt as contributing to one's image of self-esteem, of success, and of all the aspirations this image includes. Personality growth can be motivated by concern for the other, by being-for-another. This is personality in its mature becoming.

Motivation for personality development differs in one essential aspect. Negative motives may be very effective for specific actions and self-preservation. Fear of mishap may motivate people to be very cautious. The picture of an accident may make drivers more alert and cut down speeding. But for personality growth, motivation must be predominantly positive. Instilling fear in a person does not help him to become expansive. Even if he is too overt in his approaches to others, threats are not helpful. He develops more social sensitivity through love than through fear. Growth in personality, in awareness of others, depends upon motivation that unfolds, that draws an individual forward, and invites him to participate. Effective human relations will depend on motivations of love, hope, courage, and joy. With these dynamic energies dominating, the personality expands and encompasses greater diversities in others. Human relationships are fostered by whatever is communicative, not by what is inhibiting. Reciprocal exchange is free from fear and full of trust. The mature personality does not impose on another, or intrude, or infringe upon another's freedom, but shares, exchanges, and reciprocates. The mature personality in its fullness of being is motivated positively to take the risk, to make the leap—in Kierkegaard's word—that brings him to another's threshold. In the whole concept of motivation for growth, factors that encourage the outward flow of self, the continuation, the commitment, are the most appealing motivations for felt-knowledge of others.

Felt-Knowledge

As the concentric circles of experience widen, motivations deepen. What changes is the evaluating process; what served as a keen interest to the child does not appeal to the adolescent mind, and the vacillations of adolescents account for their rapid changes of interest. However, in each individual, what does not change is the need for positive self-fulfillment, and whatever he perceives as a contribution to this goal he will accept. But he must know it and be dynamically drawn to it before it will be influential for him as a motive. For example, a student may be given all of the advantages of learning a language and he may realize them very well but may not be motivated to study it. But if he meets a girl who speaks only this language and he loves her and wants to communicate, he will learn the language rapidly. The difference, of course, is the experience of love which is now attached to his realization of the advantages of a new language. At first this realization was knowledge—later motivation. The challenge in motivating ourselves or others is to introduce the purpose with some *felt-knowledge*. Without this emotional enhancement, our knowledge of a fact will not be an influential motive. The idea must be accompanied with a "glow" in order to serve as a motivation. This is the distinctly human character in motivation. The person is eventually a being who knows and feels, and he is most himself when he is functioning in this wholeness.Whatever appeals to him as a total person will be most influential.

Awareness of man's sensitivity to felt-knowledge will enlighten our approach to motivation. Effective motivation must be offered in its completeness; must be presented in a positive atmosphere, as something to be desired rather than avoided, and as something that can be known and loved. What is known but not loved usually will not be an influential motivation. Motivation must be concrete for children and also for adolescents. For an adult, motivation will vary according to maturity and personality. But the same principle will hold. An adult loves differently than an adolescent and his broader experiences increase his evaluative knowledge. But he also will be most influenced by motives suited to his capacity, which he can receive as felt-values.

This explanation of motivation is important for understanding the nature of personality. A person who has acquired habits of relating to others that are superficial, indirect, insincere, and unattractive will be motivated to change his manner only through felt-values. Telling him, sermonizing, or talking about these habits will be of little avail. His realization and joy in another's openness and stability will be much more effective. Explanations offered along with a personal knowing and feeling of another's sincerity and authenticity will be the most influential motivation of all. A person who is criticized for his behavior and at the same time experiences rejection may change his ways, but only superficially and perhaps with increased resentment which will be expressed in another direction. People do change because of threats, but not in productive ways. The change may temporarily alleviate the situation for others, may be expedient, but the deficiencies of the person himself have not been remedied. A personal change involves a risk, a loss of the old securities. The medium of fear, of rejection and hostility creates an atmosphere that stifles the risk. It induces one to hide, to avoid, to withdraw. The human person motivated through love surges forward, bridges a gap, is courageous, hazards uncertainty, modifies his personality efficaciously. The candid openness of another disarms, dissolves fears, and destroys false facades. It is the open, loving approach to another that enhances the message we hope to convey.

Chapter 3

PSYCHOLOGICAL FREEDOM

Freedom is the expression of our greatest human potential and is the chief source of uniqueness. Our physical properties are genetic in origin, determined by laws of nature. Environmental contributions to the self are numerous, but what really makes the person unique, besides the individuality of his being, is his freedom. The human person can choose this in preference to that; he can choose or not choose. In his freedom he is uniquely himself and only in this freedom can he truly grow and become. Until we have known a man in his freedom we have not known him, for we only know what he carries outside of himself. Whatever is imposed upon him, whatever framework surrounds him, is only the shell in which he is encased. All of this may be shed and still the true man remains. Only what he absorbs from without by his choices, or selects to be part of him, really becomes an aspect of himself. In this freedom lies his own greatest potential. The qualities we admire most in others arise from human freedom: dignity, nobility, courage, honesty, charity. If these qualities do not spring from freedom, they lose their meaning. A noble, courageous act is a free act. Love means a free movement toward another; honesty is a free acknowledgment.

Many cultural conventionalities are imposed on us and make strenuous demands. Some can be absorbed and freely selected, but the danger in any highly structured environment is that the individual's freedom be impeded and his human dignity reduced. The more a person's freedom diminishes, the less he is able to function as a fulfilled human being. If he is subjected entirely to the rule of another, his freedom lessens, but his dynamic flow of energy does not. His energies may be repressed and expend themselves in building resentment and hostility, or with more awareness may flow in the direction of open rebellion or force. When we are young we are taught social skills and the demands of convention in order to function as social beings. Our beginning perceptions are meager and do not distinguish clearly between fact and fancy, much less between conventional behavior and principle. In his unfolding, the person must gradually distinguish these differences; otherwise when he reaches independence he may throw off both essentials and nonessentials. Overemphasis on details leads to erroneous knowledge and in early education we may have failed to distinguish between what is "nice" and what is "right." Later we may decide that wearing gloves and a tie are not necessary for us, but we must realize that we cannot dispense with honesty or respect for another in the same way. If a child has suffered similar punishment for moral offenses and for lapses in etiquette, he fails to distinguish principle from convention and may cast both aside as useless. If he realizes the personal value of regard for others and has experienced the warmth of it from his parents or others, he will choose to cultivate it within himself. This will be the real self in its becoming, the self that internalizes the values presented when he was unable to perceive for himself. Knowing them fully through felt-relations with others, he freely incorporates them and expresses them in his unique way.

INTERNALIZATION

The human person can routinely perform many exterior functions for a long period of time without internalizing them. As external functions they can be dropped as quickly as they were initiated. Persons who adopt patterns of behavior through fear, human respect, or social prestige may also relinquish them quickly when the fear or social demands are removed. These are examples of superficial structures which the ego builds because of necessity and not through freedom. A form of behavior that bears meaning to an individual and which he freely expresses will be as permanent as its meaningfulness to him. The genuine person develops an authentic personality compatible with his inner convictions and living knowledge. He relates to others in a genuine wholehearted way because he believes in the relationship. It holds meaning for him. One forms enduring identity only through freedom, through choosing for oneself what one knows and wants, deciding and selecting the values one wants to assimilate and to identify with oneself. This formation of identity—that is, the solidarity of the person in his uniqueness—and the development of personality—the genuine person relating to others—can be realized only through freedom.

The human person cannot comprehend real responsibility or real guilt unless he has grown freely. Responsibility means freely to accept an obligation. Guilt feelings, so frequently observed in compulsive neurotics, do not result from awareness of wrong, but from unconscious hostility against impositions. A sense of freedom produces strength for responsibility, fosters courage and stability.

The self that has been built along prescribed lines imposed by convention will be a fragile, inflexible ego. The criteria for behavior will be prestige, approval, and praise. The methods of self-fulfillment will be primarily those of imitation and conformity. The processes of imitation and conformity require a constant extension and revamping; the internal self, without maturity or assurance, remains fixed and static. The exterior changes are not fundamental or meaningful and little personal growth occurs. The values are imitations of another and remain exterior to the real self. Each new situation becomes a threat because there is no foreknowledge of possibilities and no personal criterion for selection. The conformist is dependent for all of these on another. Hence his life is filled with fear of change and the threat of unexpected demands. Safety lies in sameness, and he strives to preserve this at any cost by a methodical, orderly demeanor. The human person is unable to survive for long in this way of living. Thus he begins to think and to behave as he believes others want him to think and behave. His thought and behavior do not stem from perceived values, personal convictions, meaningful ideals. This kind of existence rests on shifting grounds, brings little personal satisfaction, and leads to unrealistic living and behaving. Eventually the structure built on approval from others crumbles, and the person is prostrate with his own emptiness. Either he rids himself of the burdens of conformity, and begins over again in other surroundings the process of growth towards maturity, or he becomes estranged to the structure he has built on another's foundation where he has lost himself and his own identity. In the former, a certain overt rebellion occurs and in the latter, he is engulfed in mental disorder.

DIMENSIONS OF FREEDOM

The sense of identity, so essential for mature behavior, cannot develop in the absence of freedom, because only by expressing his real self does a person mature. As one gains more self-awareness, the span of choice widens and the need to choose is greater. With each selection the self is strengthened and equipped for more decisions. The frequent exercise of freedom widens the scope of self-extension and enables one to shoulder greater responsibilities.

For the development of maturity, freedom from self-constriction is essential: through it and by it one lives in security, meets others candidly and directly, without pretense or defense, without fear or hostility, in unity, harmony, and wholesome mutuality. As Kierkegaard indicates in his writings, one must be self-sufficient in order to truly love another (Kierkegaard, 1941).

Freedom is an aspect of love and becomes more understandable in terms of this affective movement. Love is in its essence a free movement toward an object that is known to be good. If love is not free, it has become something else, or was not love to begin with, perhaps a simulation. Each person as he experiences real love is conscious of the outgoingness of himself towards the other. He is not compelled by another force or drawn against his will, for this would be only attraction and not love. Love includes attraction but transcends it and is large and comprehensive because it is free-flowing. Freedom viewed in its affiliation with love helps us to understand its necessity for growth. Love and freedom go hand in hand in the formation of the self and the extension of self. Freedom is not the harmful dissipation of aimless energies, expending the self impulsively; not the path of license or of repression let loose in destructive outlets. Freedom is the exercise of knowledge in seeking the true, and of love seeking the good.

The human person is contingent on another for his existence. In his existence a man cannot be alone in himself. He is inevitably situated in relation to others. In the flux of his living he is surrounded by others, is one of them; and as a human being is either with another, for another, against or apart from others. Man in his active relatedness to others is man in his existential reality.

Freedom from Self

Freedom, then, stems from the person's most profound selfhood, and his freedom in relating is his essential function. When his freedom and relatedness to others are impaired, intrinsic needs are denied and he cannot perform as a person. Human freedom includes freedom from self and freedom from external coercion; the two are often intertwined. The dynamic energies are equipment for action; they are in continual process, pulsating, flowing without ceasing. Many of these movements are spontaneous, others are directed by the self. The psychic energies orient positively and negatively toward their objects. The person free in self-direction is fully aware and expends these energies in beneficial ways. Through the self-direction of his energies he attains selfhood, personalized identity, and communicates himself to others. Competent self-direction requires freedom.

Freedom from Fear

Freedom from inner compulsion, from fearfulness, anxiety, delusions, hate, and resentment, enables the self to mature and to relate to others. Freedom can be so obstructed by patterns of fear and escape dynamisms that the self cannot function in its fullest dignity as a person. The self becomes encumbered by the barriers that these dynamisms set up. The complicated maze of feelings in the neurotic and psychotic disorders demonstrate the most severe disturbances in the exercise of freedom. Mentally disordered persons have become dehumanized by their own inner restrictions. The unconscious influences dominate and overwhelm the personality and impair all human relationships. Neurotic and psychogenic disorders are primarily dynamic derangements in which self-direction has been reduced to a minimum, while hyperactive emotions and repressions have usurped control. The coordinated expressions of the unified self disintegrate and the human person is less able to function. His fears, aggressions, and hostility take precedence over everything and his actions are compelled by these movements. The domination of fear and hostility curtails the person in all of his relationships with others because these reactions evaluate all in terms of self. Regression draws the person more and more away from others, back into the infantile world from which he had emerged, into the helplessness and inertness of a complete self-absorption.

Impediments to freedom from self range from minor egoistic habits to the major problems caused by neuroses and psychoses. Habits such as daydreaming, worrisome attitudes, defensive and escape dynamisms tend to cause a haphazard dissipation of internal energies. These are the small impediments that curtail freedom. To be what he wants to be, to seek the goals he desires to achieve, to attain, to love and to enjoy fully, the person must be free from himself to move outward. Energies wastefully expended within are enfeebled in outward expression. The human person is fulfilled only in love and joy and he attains these only when he is free enough from within to extend himself outward to others. In his aloneness, in his inward isolation he is completely empty, frustrated, and miserable. In his freedom to relate, to love, to be courageous, to enjoy, he is exercising his humanness and the dignity of his being. Whatever enables a man to be free from inner constrictions releases his nobility which is concealed beneath his repressions.

THE FREEDOM TO LOVE

Freedom as an aspect of love refers to the unimpeded movement of the self towards another. Love is formed within and is a free act of the human person which no one else can prevent. Love can be intercepted in its expression by external circumstances but can never be forestalled by an external intermediary. It is an intrinsic act of the human person. But other internal states, such as hate, fear, and anger can strike at the very process of love and hinder or change its course. When freedom is deterred either by internal conditions or external restraints, hate, the direct opposite of love, is born. When the freedom of a human person is fettered, the energy of love is reversed and turns into hate. The dynamic energies intrinsic to the person in his becoming may be positive or negative in their direction, and there will always be one direction that dominates. Hate, fear, and resentment spring from deprivations of freedom and limitations of self-actualization which the individual develops only in the world of otherness. He is independent as this being, but his existential reality always includes his being related to others. He is dependent, then, on others for self-fulfillment, because he cannot love unless there is someone to love and he cannot be free unless he moves toward others. The very nature of freedom implies movement toward others. He cannot be open, ready, eager, and outgoing to *nothing*. There is always something to which one's freedom relates. Each person, then, is more or less involved in the freedom of others, directly or indirectly. To understand the nature of hate and resentment we must be aware of factors that restrict freedom since the origins of these energies will always be relevant to some interference with the emergence of the self.

IMPEDIMENTS TO FREEDOM

Hate and aversion have their normal developmental roles and can be helpful to the individual in his selections. Aversion to impediments to growth, hatred for undesirable habits, help to eliminate these handicaps. Hate, aversion, fear, and anger become destructive when they are excessive, when they outweigh the growth processes, when they are hidden in unconscious repressions. In neurotic and psychotic personalities, negative dynamics are dominant and consuming. The ego is stripped of freedom and is enslaved by the tyranny of energies which dispel themselves in many directions without reason or purpose. When a person cannot fulfill himself, cannot relate to others, or does so feebly, he is overwhelmed with frustration and depression. In the mental disorders the person's freedom is so handicapped that he cannot be himself, he cannot relate normally, and his status as an actualized human being is severely reduced. In these states we see the anarchy of negative dynamics in full sway and the limitations of freedom in an extreme degree.

Freedom is as necessary to the development of the personality as food is for the growth of the body. In the normal course of events each person meets resistance, experiences hate and aversion, knows fear and discouragement, suffers resentment and hostility. While the positive emotions mold, amplify, and augment, the negative emotions prevent, stifle, and eradicate. It is the balanced interplay that accomplishes self-actualization. And the dominance of love, joy, and courage widens the flow toward creative and renewing formations. It is the restriction of intrinsic freedom which allows hate and resentment to dominate.

A government, a way of life, a job that encroaches on the intrinsic freedom of the human person stimulates hate and resentment. To understand the accumulation of hate and hostility we need to know the restrictions of freedom involved. A man may work in a factory because he couldn't find another job. His choice is not entirely free and his acceptance halfhearted. If his boss is overbearing and demanding, hate and resentment will soon fester within him. His tolerance of this undesirable situation will depend upon the satisfaction of his other human relationships, his survival needs, and his opportunities for wholesome outlets. If he meets too much opposition, he will be inefficient and careless in his work. But the hate and resentment he experiences in these circumstances will lessen his openness to others and retard his own fulfillment. Many people are caught like this in the demands of industry and depersonalizing mechanizations. The effects on personality are deadening and account for many mental disorders. We spontaneously react against any curbing or thwarting of our personal inner growth, perhaps by frustration or anger. Delinquency too, is often an outer thrust against an inner stifling of growth caused by oppressive circumstances.

POSITIVE RELATIONSHIPS ARE FREE

Effective interpersonal relationships and genuine mutuality depend on the freedom of each person. It is the restriction one person places on another that causes hate and resentment. Openness of mind, largeness of spirit, the willingness to let another person be himself, gives him a sense of freedom, and is a gesture of love. We spontaneously move toward those who are open, receptive, and welcoming. We recoil from those who are threatening, domineering, and rejecting. People will be unable to relate to others if they are denied the opportunities of self-expression, or of participation and sharing. Positive interpersonal relationships are built on dialogue, on interchange, on rapprochement, all of which recognize human freedom. To clear the air of hostility, to rid the situation of hate and resentment, there must be renewed presence, awareness of human dignity, and a mutual exercise of freedom. When a person offers himself to the other as a responsive being, he offers him love and the freedom to be. To relate to another effectively, one must be something *to* him and *for* him. All human interchange, no matter how superficial or temporary, requires mutual recognition of dignity and freedom. The man who serves others in the humblest tasks must receive in return the freedom and dignity due his intrinsic worth. Otherwise, hate and rebellion mount within him.

In every human endeavor, beginning with the activities of the young child, through adolescence to adulthood, the exercise of freedom is necessary to avert hate and resentment. The child who cannot make decisions in his own limited realm becomes a hostile child. The adolescent whose parents select his clothes and choose his vocation, grows daily in resentment. The adult who is given a job to do and allowed no freedom of execution and who must operate like a robot grows rebellious and dissatisfied. Freedom is not license, dissipation, or haphazard, aimless activity, or lack of discipline; it is opposed to all of these, though often confused with some. The person who has experienced freedom chooses, selects, becomes responsible. He is disciplined because he has known opportunities for self-direction. He grows toward maturity because he grows in love; he relates to others because he is free from dominating hatred, resentment, and fear. He remains free from pretense, recognizes his selfhood and enriches his personality in its continuation.

Chapter 4

DEVELOPMENTAL STAGES
OF PERSONALITY

INFANCY

Personality emerges from the growth in communication beginning from the child's entrance into the world. From the time of his birth he begins the slow, continual evolvement which leads him to adult relationships. Personality is not a particular goal that is reached at a set period of time, but the person's power to communicate, developed sufficiently to relate maturely to other human beings. The child from the moment of his existence stands in relationship to others as a new being, and at his birth is distinctly this social being on the threshold of life. Relatedness has begun, is emitted through cries and gestures, blends into words and actions, and eventually becomes the complicated system of rapprochement with others which is the personality.

The social needs issuing from man's essential nature are the quintessence of human communication. These inherent needs form the basic dynamics from which flow the lifelong rhythm of need and fulfillment. The person wants to be accepted and understood, to be loved, to belong, and to achieve. He is dependent on others for these needs, and, in receiving, he becomes able to impart what others need from him. His existence is a constant search for fulfillment and his maturity lies in giving and being for others. All through the life span of the individual he seeks to express and to communicate according to his level of development. But at each chronological stage, these particular needs are manifested in distinctly different patterns of communication. To recognize the cues requires an awareness of feeling as it varies in expression at different age levels.

The newborn infant embraces the potentials of his whole existence but lies helpless in his crib, completely dependent on others for survival and continuation. Even at birth his psychological nature is more delicate than his body, and he can survive longer without food than without affection. His need for acceptance is so vital that the lack of it for any noticeable time in his infancy will weaken his psychological and physical stamina. Modern research has discovered autism in infants who were reared without normal love and affection. An infant, well-fed and clothed, but left alone for long periods of time will soon become apathetic and listless. His need for assurance and for complete acceptance is acute and with each renewal of love he gains strength and reaches out to his environment. In his tiny frame he contains unpredictable latencies which burgeon little by little each day. Lying side by side with many others in the same nursery, hardly distinguishable from them by the casual onlooker, he is completely individual, and perhaps potentially poles apart from his neighbors. The embarrassment of the new father who cannot recognize his own newborn child in the hospital nursery is a good example of the uniqueness which exists unquestionably, but which lies dormant in the infant.

The infant's need to communicate and know response is intense. He soon begins to discover means of drawing the attention of others and each success is followed by renewed attempts. His need for response helps him to cry, to babble, to make noises of all kinds with his mouth, hands, and feet. Through responses to these primitive beginnings the child is accepted, loved, and understood.

Preschool Children

Later the child communicates through things and he grasps objects and manipulates them. From this time on until adulthood the child's chief mode of communication is through the medium of play. The adult will never know a child until he has played with him. The more he enters into the play world of the child, speaks to him through the language of play, the more intimately he comes to know him. It is in his play particularly that the child understands others. He expresses himself most spontaneously in the endless constructions he builds, the toys he pushes around and the objects he loves and fondles. He cannot communicate much directly because his world is composed of things. His perceptions and instincts predominate and we must meet him on his own ground. Children talk to one another through play. They share and fight over toys, push and pull things together, gesticulate and grimace. They sit together to draw or paint. Two children rarely sit down together and just talk or chat: for them this is an estrangement. They wouldn't know what to say because things, gestures, exchange in play, are their media rather than words.

Rhythmic Games

The child continues to be more interested in things than in other people and is asocial in his behavior. He prefers to have people around him but is not particularly interested in playing with others for long periods of time. His desire for the company of others is spasmodic and he abandons it quickly for solitary play. Later he begins to socialize through more definite kinds of play. The preschool child is exhilarated at joining others for rhythmic games. In his energy and endurance for physical exertion in these amusements he often outstrips his adult partner. Rhythmic play is the young child's favorite way of socializing and through these games he learns a little give and take quickly because the rhythmic gestures have such strong appeal. Dancing with another in rhythmic steps, he feels free and open. Parents can communicate their own receptivity, warmth, and reassurance by swinging along with their children in these games. The delight of children as they dance along with a parent overflow into shrieks of gaiety.

Representative Play

Representative play is another favorite of the preschool child who is so frequently seen promenading in adult clothes and shoes, imitating the mannerisms and words of his parents. The whole gamut of fantasy is dramatized and played out. Hours are passed in playing teacher and school, parents with the family, the storekeeper in buying and selling. What is primary in this period is the imitation of adult habits. Children repeat the phrases they hear over and over again with perfect imitation and inflections. They quickly absorb the feelings demonstrated by adults and adopt them as their own. On the other hand, children who witness the phobias, tantrums, and selfishness of adults begin to make them a part of their own fantasy. In their play they often act out the aggressions and hostilities they have perceived in their parents. Through play of this kind the preschool child reveals his feelings and the early tendencies of dynamic patterns. He communicates to others more through gestures than words. Verbalizations are too complicated and sparse. His range of feelings is far greater than his vocabulary and his ability to speak much too limited to show others his real self. He spontaneously resorts to action to communicate to another and the response of gesture is more meaningful to him than words. The child who is overwhelmed by fear or hunger remains speechless. In his deepest sufferings a child is incapable of speech and often incapable of tears. He may become fixed and motionless, a truly pathetic sight. In his natural, wholesome development the child sparkles with alertness, is spontaneous and happy, moving in every direction with carefree ease.

Play and Activity

Pure action for the sake of action is also the young child's sport. He finds sheer pleasure in running back and forth in open spaces, in sliding down muddy slopes, rolling on the turf, tumbling and turning, jumping and stamping. The free exercise of all the large muscles, grown strong, animates his whole body and he darts hither and yon without heed of others. But this is his way of communicating to the outside world, of giving himself to others. In his physical movement, rhythmical dance, gestures, imitations, and play he offers himself to others. When another meets him, joins him, plays with him, dances with him, he expresses his love in a way best understood by the child. Verbal phrases of love mean little to the child unless they are accompanied by an understanding of his active, rhythmic, representative play.

Painting and Drawing

A child communicates easily through drawing and painting. He delights in splashing paint on paper with flat brushes, or scribbling with crayons. He instinctively identifies colors with his feelings and through them conveys his moods. Colors combined with lines and forms reveal the child's subjective world. His intense feelings and dispositions find an easy outlet in painting. The freedom of using any color he wishes, of moving his arms in circles if he feels happy, or in making broad harsh strokes if he is hostile gives him relief and he can ventilate readily. Through painting, scribbling, and coloring he externalizes himself and achieves a certain strength in his own productions. He often pours out a whole sequence of fantasy in his use of colors, lines, and shapes. He can paint his anger in red and then cover it up with blue if he wants. He can draw a picture of his family and put his dad in the corner if he is angry with him. He can draw himself and put a big hat on if he wants to be tall and important. The child can create marvels for himself in his painting and objectify his feelings with facility.

And besides helping him to know and understand his feelings, painting gives him a certain sensitivity to line and color and he feels at home with them. He can harmonize and flow along with the rise and fall of lines on the page and the smooth mixture of colors. The child's attachment to his scribbles and free painting shows how closely he identifies with them. He holds them sacred because they are very much himself and he feels close to people who look at them and admire them with attention. He cannot tolerate a misinterpretation of his work, someone else's projection into his drawing. But he derives much satisfaction from another's affectionate interest in his products. He points out different figures and events in the colors or the crisscross of lines which are obscure for adults. Many significant features are symbolized by the hodgepodge he presents to another. The weary father who slumps into his armchair after a full day of hard work may find it difficult to see beauty in the messy paper thrust before him. But his acceptance and interest in the offer is the warmest kind of affection he can give to the child.

Through all of these various forms of nonverbal relatedness the child reveals himself and tries to enter into the beingness of others. We must receive him and respond to him in these attempts; otherwise he feels shut off from adults, unloved by others. This is the language which the child understands best and through it ventures to press forward and find new sources. In this way he orients to higher levels of discovering others; relatedness to others does not begin suddenly but proceeds from a long line of events. The child who has not fully enjoyed these opportunities to expend himself will be impoverished and will lack the early beginnings of strong identity. The negative responses from his parents for long periods of time and the scarcity of opportunities for these forms of play may impair the formations which prepare him to progress in his outward relatedness. All of these preliminary stages fashion the self, give it firmness, and increase its security in the world of being-with-others. Being-in-the-world is not a threat but a joy, an exciting adventure. This is the normal expectancy of the child who has received love and warmth in the ways he understands best.

Children demonstrate more vividly imaginative sources since they are unable to verbalize. Gestures and play are more indirect methods, more symbolic, but constitute the level of communication when words are deficient. In these first attempts of the child to relate to another we are reminded forcefully of the inutility of words and phrases for certain occasions. Even as the child attains more verbal proficiency the nonverbal approaches do not cease. Gradually they recede to the background but remain throughout the life cycle.

Later Childhood

A day arrives when the child sees the rhythmic games as funny or silly and looks with scorn upon his younger brother and sister playing house. He cannot find himself in this domain any longer. He has passed on to newer and more attractive realms. He seeks a more realistic setting and his interests draw him toward other outlets. His speech patterns have changed markedly and he converses with greater facility, but speech is still not his preferred mode of communication. His play includes more verbalizations, more meaningful objects, but he is still primarily concerned with his own imaginative world.

Collections

He is absorbed in things, fascinated with their structure and their mechanisms. His sensory perceptions take on new dimensions. He watches and observes everything with intensity. He likes the feel of things and in a sense becomes a part of them. He likes to have things and manipulates them as his very own. He expends a great part of his energy in gathering and collecting objects that are often useless but hold an irresistible attraction for him. He relentlessly accumulates objects of his fancy and stores them with great care. He examines them by the hour and shares them only with trusted admirers. His collections may include sundry trinkets: bottle tops, dead butterflies, seashells, rocks, plastic soldiers, knives. Almost any object can become the child's delight. He is earthbound and in his contact with things discovers in them a certain "mystic" quality. The enchantment which he realizes in these odds and ends is often beyond the comprehension of adults. His bewildered parents often survey the accumulation of junk in his bedroom and wonder what to do about it. Their astuteness in handling this delicate problem in human relationships will indicate their ability to communicate with him. A hasty disposal of the inconvenient trash may put barriers between them and the child. This lack of insight may damage bonds of affection and desirable interchange. On the other hand, a certain interest in the peculiar storehouse and a willingness to participate in the intriguing play of the child as he sorts and resorts, covers and uncovers his treasures, will enlighten the perplexity of his parents and lead them into his world. Through his miscellaneous assortments he can voice his feelings, dreams, and fantasies. Through his world of collections his parents come to know him well. He experiences warmth from their interest, and in a marvelous way, by this attention from his parents he is able to mature and outgrow his need for these miscellaneous assortments. Deprived of affection he will clutch onto things and not be able to rise above them. Only when he has lived securely in this realm is he able to emerge from it.

Competition

The young schoolchild resorts to various forms of competition through tussling, disputing, and fighting. He learns through these concrete means the individual rights of others and that he cannot transgress them. He wants to associate with others but must learn to give in order to receive respect. He edges himself forward, meets others, engages in physical conflicts and better understands certain rules of conduct. His preferred play is competitve. He wants to fight and win, to accept challenge and to try his wings. Games of group or individual competition are high among his interests. Many end in disputes and disorder, only to begin all over again another day. The psychological satisfaction at this stage is just as keen in the actual competition as it is in the end result. That is why the young child seldom wearies of disputes in baseball games, or time lost in deciding who is going to bat first. For him, this is a satisfying part of the game. An adult who wants to watch a game is impatient with the ceaseless wranglings of small children over the details that impede the actual performance. But the young child thrives on these minor conflicts. Through these exchanges he learns many vital standards of behaving: rules of fair play, sharing with others, respect for free enterprise, sportsmanship, and team cooperation. He learns the rudimentary facts of social living in meaningful situations.

Fighting becomes a part of the child's play activity. He maneuvers many situations at home and at school to stir a little commotion. He nudges his neighbor, pushes another, bumps into his friends, yanks the hair of the girl in front of him, more out of a desire to be with someone than because of hostility. The insecure child will often be hurtful in his fighting, but for most children it is another way of relating. He needs the chance to compete often in small tasks; this is his language. Adults cannot enter directly into the combat between children but they do so by a certain balanced tolerance for their dissensions. Constructive kinds of rivalry eliminate aggression and open a positive course for the expenditure of energy. The angry retorts of parents or unreasonable resistance to children's competitive spirits can quickly change their fun into belligerence. Lack of opportunity for wholesome competing leads a child to cultivate habits of resentful thinking and unconscious hate.

Love for Plants and Animals

The child sometimes finds it easier to show his feelings to animals and plants than to human beings. He finds them intensely interesting and he enjoys reading about them, discovering all the intricacies of their habitats and the peculiarities of each species. He likes to watch everything move and grow. He is captivated by young animals with whom he identifies in their dependence and need for care and protection. He loves to nurture small animals and becomes fiercely attached to them. He learns to relate to ordinary objects first and then to living things which require more personal care and attention. This stage is a necessary link and stepping-stone to a real concern for other people. A pet animal can become the object of a child's personal ownership and he learns to think in terms of life to be safeguarded, sustained, and fed. The child who is cruel to animals is often mentally disturbed, for if his development has been wholesome, he is normally very protective of them.

In his regard for plants and animals he exercises gentleness and acquires a tenderness that tempers the rough edges of his competitive spirit. These two vigorous tendencies complement one another. They prepare the child to meet other persons with a similar combination of self-respect and sympathetic solicitude. In these early contacts with otherness the child initiates habits that take root in opportunities of expression. If he is continually opposed in his attempts at self-expression he becomes frustrated and resorts to negative behavior. If he never experiences an attachment for an animal, never knows the joy of playing with a pet, never helps a plant grow, he will have difficulty later in being compassionate and sympathetic with others. Omissions and gaps in childhood are lost opportunities for the future and will require compensation. For the child, the time to play is the chance to "become" and to learn how to live with others. Play is the child's life, and many decisive measures for his future originate in play. Adults who go along with children in their escapades with pets, tedious though they may be, will always be able to influence them. The child never forgets a cruelty shown to his pet. An adult who intentionally ignores a child's love for his possessions has lost touch with the real feelings of the child. The child becomes impenetrable to someone he considers a ruthless intruder.

Emulation

The child's span of attention is limited and his qualitative comprehension of words is more limited than the same vocabulary in adult usage. He learns a very small amount from verbal instructions or admonitions. He will not grasp these in the full adult context; moreover, he easily tires listening to others, especially if he is forced to do so for any length of time. He assimilates the meanings of virtue or desirable conduct more through stories and example than through conversation. A child must enter into the spirit of an entire situation, see the characters in his imagination and feel the reality. When he emulates what he admires he does so with all his imitative resources. He walks, talks, breathes the air of his hero, lives the adventure in his fantasy and acts it out frequently. He enters into this new world of adventure or story of courage and cannot view it simply as an onlooker. When the child esteems a famous character he adopts him as a model and imitates him in many details. Through emulation of this kind he learns best the meaning of virtue. He learns to be sensitive to others and he begins to move toward greater maturity.

A story told, written, or vividly portrayed on his level imparts impressively what a sermon or a talk never could. The child is inspired more permanently by what he sees and hears at the same time. Acts of courage or valor which he personally witnesses stir him to imitate the same. He strives to become his ideal by imitating these externals. At the same time he absorbs some of the meanings implied in his hero's actions. Vivid examples in real-life situations fill him with strong desires to seek the same experiences within his own framework. Virtues and social standards are internalized through his tendency to imitate; it is one of his chief modes of communication. These qualities imprinted upon him as praiseworthy will be revealed through his dramatizations in play. The role he assumes most often in play is the one that has impressed him the most. Historical figures a child comes to know in pleasant surroundings will penetrate his motivational system. In school, he will value the historical figures who demonstrate nobility of character if he has learned about them with eagerness and interest. Otherwise, these heroes of the past may symbolize nothing more than a tiresome and dull teacher.

Through these dynamic tendencies which dominate his thinking and perceiving, the young child extends himself in his contacts with others. His parents and other associates, in turn, accept him, show warmth, and communicate profoundly. The child cannot grasp meanings in an adult context, and he relies entirely on the resources corresponding to his period of development. Competition, emulation, imitation, ownership, and affinity for animals are most significant for him and he must first receive understanding through these channels in order to move forward to other ways of relating.

Without these opportunities to grow, he will acquire undesirable patterns of behavior. He will have problems and be confused if he is socially immature in his age group. The young child becomes more and more social, seeks status and prestige among his companions as well as in his home. Children are keenly perceptive and easily see social inadequacies in their playmates. Their judgments of each other are hard and unyielding; they tend to ostracize or shun members of their group who demonstrate deficiencies in social rapport. The demands for give

and take increase with age, and the child who has not had sufficient opportunities for maturation in the early states, later becomes lost in the pressures of the group and feels cut off and
very alone. He doesn't know how to play with others and is un-
happy because his need to be with the group is increasingly intense. Communicating to him in meaningful ways will avoid
these problems and enable him to participate actively in his own
age group.

ADOLESCENCE

Gradually and imperceptibly the young child disengages
himself from his sundry collections and looks upon them as
uninteresting trifles. The captivating enchantment has left
them, and the child in becoming a youth is drawn by other attractions. He has merged into the group, not in the competitive
role that he held before, but as an integral part, a constituent of
the whole. His ideas and feelings blend with those of his companions and he feels one with them. This group unity is predominately a unity of feeling and the youth does not examine
the situation before he enters it. On the contrary, through feelings he falls into line with those with whom he finds an affinity.
Adolescent groups are not formed on judgments and reasonings.
Environmental factors bring some of them together, but kinship
of feeling which they intuit in one another is the bond of union
among them. The similarity of dynamic needs knits them together; in other respects—physical, economic, intellectual—the
group may contain a motley mixture.

Group Identity

Adolescents tend to adopt group standards and ideals instead of those of their parents. The strength of affectional bonds
already established with their parents will determine the amount
of parental influence during adolescence. Even at best, the
group acceptance looms high in the adolescent's mind. The
group is his natural milieu and within it he finds the most satisfaction for dynamic needs so intense within him. The need for

relating to others by participation reaches a certain height in this phase of his unfolding. In order to reach adult status, which follows this period of development, he requires many opportunities to exercise his ego strength and gain sufficient independence to maintain himself. In the adolescent group he feels at home and experiences the kind of otherness that satisfies. His parents and family do not suffice; he finds his greatest solace in the immediate company of his friends. He sees himself in them and identifies closely. The same interests, feelings, and sentiments prevail, and all are very remote from those of adults. Adult thinking holds a certain repugnance for the adolescent; it appears removed, pedantic, colorless, and obsolete. At times, adolescents have even described strong feelings of disgust for some adults. It is the group that has verve, resiliency, and encompasses all the challenges for excitement and thrills. Just the feeling of vibrating with the group fills the adolescent with exhilaration.

In identifying with the group he adopts the predominant modes of expression, whatever they may be. It makes no difference what he wears as long as it conforms to the group's standards: the need for money and possessions depends on the group. These essentials enable him to be one with the others. If the leaders have bikes, then he must also have one; if their possessions include stereos, cars, and other expensive items, he strives to maintain prestige by having the same. When he is unable to be like the others or maintain status he meets difficult problems and seeks to compensate. Group pressures are strenuous and adolescents are continually in the process of changing and adapting to keep step with the tempo of the crowd. By identification with the group, adolescents make their first attempt to sever themselves from their parents and to gain independence. They are too insecure as individuals to stand apart from their parents and they experience a strong ambivalence; but in the group they feel reassured by the companionship they find, and they move away from parental dominance into the group where they feel free but not alone. The adolescent must move into the group to feel secure, and in it he exchanges and grows independent; later he moves out of it in the assurance of his own selfhood.

Cooperation

The desire for close social living with peers gives the adolescent a special yen for cooperative effort. He is happiest when he is working, playing, living with the group, and will contribute his best to a cause endorsed by his group. Civic projects and school enterprises sponsored by adolescent groups are executed with enthusiasm and usually with admirable success. Undertakings of this kind are mutually beneficial. Opportunities to cooperate also emphasize the adolescent's finest qualities. Pledged to group endeavors, adolescents can accomplish wonders and in the process, they themselves mature. Together they can exercise generosity, self-sacrifice, and courage. But if they were to attempt activities alone, their self-consciousness would probably handicap them. Given frequent occasions for joint undertakings, they expand their energy in positive achievements from which they derive personal dynamic satisfaction. The adolescent is quickly bored by tasks he is required to perform by himself. Even in academic learning he profits most from socialized endeavors. The adolescent way of learning is not that of the adult. Usually adults do not have the same need for learning, achieving, and working in unison. Adult social needs differ qualitatively from those of adolescents.

In cooperative efforts the adolescent can best develop his interpersonal relations. The more opportunities he has to mix in groups, to give and receive from his companions, and to join with them in working for some worthy goal, the more possibilities he has to acquire personality integration. His success as an accepted and approved member of the group has decisive effects on his attainment of maturity. In working together with his companions, he learns how to relate to others in many different situations: on the team, in clubs, social activities, academic affairs. The subjective experiences he acquires form the attitudes he maintains toward others in his adult living.

Interpersonal relationships reach a peak in adolescence because they coincide with independent reflection. The adolescent does not rely on imitation for his ideals and goals, but reasons and reflects independently of his parents and teachers. He depends on his parents for affection and support, but not for reflective thinking. He is influenced by the family environment but seeks individual status. The chances given him by his parents to increase his independence in wholesome measures will be a valuable contribution to his sense of responsibility. The adolescent does not feel responsible for the needs of his parents when he is controlled by their domination and direction. Only when he is free enough from his parents, is independent enough to see them in the perspective of his own independent responsibility, does he show consideration and thoughtfulness for them. Lack of unselfish parental love, and either tyrannical control or indifference account for most adolescent irresponsibility. The adult's openness to others, readiness to share, depends much on the opportunities for cooperative living he has known as an adolescent.

Adolescent "Mystique"

In his pursuit for independence the adolescent acquires certain mannerisms which often become quite obnoxious to adults who guide him. He adopts an attitude that reveals his desire for secretiveness. He relinquishes the talkative behavior he had as a child and assumes a noncommunicative air. For days at a time he is content to respond to his family in monosyllables and often with a shrug of shoulders or a mumbled, "I don't know." In contrast, he indulges in prolonged conversations with his friends on the telephone and resents fiercely any inquiry about them. Parents are confused by his noncommital attitude toward them and paradoxical eagerness to converse with his companions. His apparent indifference to them is too frequently interpreted as a personal affront instead of understood as his need to move into other realms of relatedness. Adult reactions of suspicion to his secretive style enkindle resistance and quarrelsomeness and often end in breaches injurious to both sides.

The adolescent revels in discussing everything and anything with his friends. But at the same time he enhances his importance in his family by enveloping all his affairs in an esoteric aura. He demands respect from others by exacting meticulous regard for his privacy. Usually his affairs which are surrounded with such mystery are unimportant in themselves, but the adolescent's intense need to be understood as an individual with self-respect is expressed in this manner. When he suffers affronts or angry rebukes from others because of this aloofness, he feels insulted and estranged. Tolerance for this exhibition of resistance toward adult domination is rewarding and the adolescent seeks the confidence of those who are able to accept him during this phase of becoming.

Argumentative Behavior

The adolescent's method of relating to adults is very different from his approach to his friends. When he communicates with parents and teachers, his favorite technique is argumentation. As a child he imitated what he liked; as an adolescent he argues about what interests him. Through argumentation he tests and tries all the goals and ideals which he finds before him. He accepts very little on faith and he submits proposed values to the rigors of reason. For most ideas or facts presented to him, either in the classroom or in the home, he demands a treatise on their validity. He argues endlessly, sometimes logically, sometimes not.

For the adolescent, it is not the right answer to the argument that is more important, but rather the argument itself. The discourse, the pros and cons, the debate of ideas give the adolescent pleasure. He delights in entrapping others in verbal disputes and the exercise of his reasoning abilities affords him much amusement. The adolescent usually argues with adults he likes, though often he annoys them and arouses their antagonism. If they view it as a hostile gesture, parents and teachers find the argumentative spirit of adolescents very difficult to endure. Actually, argumentation is the adolescent's attempt to be accepted equally as an adult by others whom he esteems. But his natural awkwardness and insecurity make him aggressive in his manner and consequently irksome. Parents and teachers who can accept the adolescent on this basis, who can temper his absurd interpretations rather than condemn him, can influence him the most. In argumentations he tries to be regarded as an adult because he cannot compete in other ways. He has no real independence from adults, socially or economically, so he unconsciously resorts to verbal haranguings to assert himself in their presence. He instinctively resents the superiority of adults and tries to outwit them in argumentation. For the adolescent, victory lies not in convincing others of his exaggerated proposals but in stirring them to pay attention to his display of wit. The adults who can skillfully manage to listen attentively to these exhortations without entering into useless opposition are the persons who will gain the adolescent's confidence. He seeks and needs recognition from adults as an individual in his own right and he attempts to show self-assertion by arguing.

The exercise of mental prowess is the way an adolescent also sounds out the reliability of adults. As he reaches later adolescence, he needs to confide in others and accepts counsel only from persons he can trust. He often approaches a teacher or a parent in a casual manner and talks about trivia before he ventures to confide in him. To help an adolescent, it is often necessary first to listen to ramblings and palaver on many topics in order to give him the assurance of a sympathetic listener. His first approaches are always in company with others. At home he will argue or hold forth on many topics in front of others for the purpose of sizing up his parents' reaction. In school he always brings two or three friends with him when he first talks to teachers and counselors. Until an adolescent is sure of his footing, he is reluctant to speak openly to an adult in a private interview. He prefers company when he chats or soliloquizes and waits until he is protected by the presence of others before drawing attention to himself. This tentative reach for contact with adults is an indication of the adolescent's awareness of adult thinking and standards. At this turning point of life when adolescence is on the threshold of young adulthood, those with whom he enjoys confidential exchanges will be the most influential in guiding his future attitudes and standards of conduct.

The personal center of the individual comes into existential reality after a long period of fundamental changing. Little by little, through the receptivity of others, the child becomes a full person. When the self has attained stature, is self-possessed and self-reliant, a person branches outward. The inner glance is no longer satisfied with the ego itself and seeks to give and be for others. In this outgoing reach the personality in its fullness has begun. When the preliminary developmental processes have been completed, personality commences, moves toward mutuality, is enriched and enjoys encounter. The personality continues and expands in renewed relationship with others by reforming and by realizing new values in interpersonal exchanges and finally achieves self-actualization in encounter and commitment.

Chapter 5

MEANINGFUL COMMUNICATION

The counselor is a communicator. He provides the necessary attitudes and situation for the client to exchange with him. Authentic communication requires the ability of one individual to enter into the perceptual world of the other. In order to understand the subjective dimensions of another person, such as his emotions and feelings, we must understand something about the stages of development through which this person has moved. If one wants to communicate to a three-year old child he must do so through the child's mentality. The preschool child is unable to comprehend the percptual world of an adult because he does not have the experience or mental equipment to do so. The same is true for a ten-year-old, an adolescent, and for some adults. Effective communication depends upon a keen awareness of a wide area of maturity levels, cultural differences and, above all, the essence of human personality.

Counseling is basically geared toward unifying mental dynamics within the person which have been diminished, alienated, or reduced. Counseling is healing and healing is integrating. Understanding the nature of personality is the first requisite in counseling. What is personality? What happens within the personality when the client is overwhelmed with anxiety? What happens within the personality when the client feels relief, when he experiences healing?

In the counseling experience it is only through encounters that these questions are answered; it is within the counseling encounter that changes take place, that the client is able to know some relief within his disturbed self. As the counselor communicates his own supportive attitudes to the client he provides a climate of warmth and acceptance that is indispensable for the healing process. As the client releases his negative, hurtful feelings to the counselor, and the counselor, in turn, accepts all, regardless of any outpouring of hostility, fear, or hatred that the client projects, the beginnings of encounter occur. It is this kind of bond, this kind of exchange which constitutes the nature of encounter. It is a giving and receiving, in a way that the client is able to let go of his painful feelings without rejection from another. In this kind of positive experience the client is gradually able to free himself from blinding emotional impediments and to begin to perceive, to feel, and to know the wholeness and mental health his entire person craves.

INTERPERSONAL COMMUNICATION

Personality, as we have seen, is the capacity of the human person to relate to others, and the unique patterns of activities formed in relating to others constitute the nature of personality. Maturity in human personality is achieved in encounter. Fullness of being is the inner movement of this individual toward others, another, the other. Encounter is extension of the inner self beyond the limits of symbols, though perhaps aided by them, to the inner self of another. The inner self is uniquely this self and no other and includes a total unity ever in flux, becoming and growing, but maintaining the core oneness of self. Encounter is specifically a human experience and exists only in the meeting of two persons. Things, places, plants, animals, and spirits of the dead cannot truly enter into encounter. Relationships exist with inanimate objects and other animate beings, but encounter is more than relationship alone. It is a specific kind of relationship existing between two human beings. Encounter is a state of being, is being in communication, is being in a reciprocal knowing and sharing.

The most difficult process to describe in the realm of human communication is the process of encounter. The most significant experience of all is meeting another. It is essential to know and to be known. One's social nature stems from essence, and both essence and fullness of being demand social interchange. Immersed in a world of objects, surrounded by many useful and necessary items he employs but which never satisfy or fulfill, the human person continually searches beyond for more internalized exchange.

INFANT NEEDS

The beginnings of communication are rooted in the first emerging consciousness of infancy where dynamic movements begin in vague, nebulous ways. In potential they are limitless, but in actuality blurred and formless, reaching out in every direction. Objects are confused in these early beginnings, but not mistaken for human responses. No matter how undeveloped the physical structure may be, the inner need for others is profound. There is a constant reaching outward especially for what satisfies and fufills, and in this early stage of awareness needs are strong but simple. The human organism instinctively moves toward otherness as a source of growth.

Soon shapes and forms become more distinct and sensations merge into more definite perceptual experiences delineated one from the other. Things are no longer perceived in global masses but rather separated into categories and entities. Some things are heard, others can be tasted and felt, still others seen and smelled. Not all are known entirely, but at least are comprehended in their exterior nature as objects, as things existing outside the self.

A CHILD RELATES TO OTHERS

These are primary experiences and form preliminary steps to relating of all kinds. These are the source materials, the early roots that make communication possible. The first stages are many and important because they produce a readiness and an openness to investigate all that is outside the organism. Little by little, the seeking for response takes on new dimensions. The child relates to others, but always in a way that pertains to himself as the pivotal figure. In his mind's eye, others surround him and he brings them to himself. He moves toward those who come to him, who serve him, who benefit him, who please him. Others remain on the fringe like shadows in the darkness.

As the growth cycle advances, the child meets his peers whom he esteems, and he gives in order to receive. Social interchange helps him to learn and absorb the objects of his desires and pursuits. He sees much about him that he wishes to possess for himself, to consume and make his own. He wants to be what he has not yet reached, and he feels that his peers participate in what he seeks, and they become vital to his increase in being, to his self-extension. He must extend himself in order to grow, and extension is meaningless unless it is directed to others. Objects do not suffice in themselves, but persons are necessary and useful, and in these periods of maturation the child seeks others instinctively. Through all these various developmental stages of relating, the child becomes himself, moving gradually toward the stature of a total person.

Many different kinds of relationships evolve in this becoming. There are relationships to parents, to family, to neighbors, workaday people, to passersby and, most important of all, to those who form the nucleus of companions. These co-partners in many enterprises, in games of all kinds, in projects, school affairs, excursions, initiate opportunities for sharing. Each relationship includes nuances and shades of relatedness differing significantly from one another. Confusions in relationships arise; some persist, some disappear, some linger always in the background, at times retarding new attempts and at other times warding off instinctive movements. Frustrations and failures are frequent and many attempted relations never occur, or are broken in the process, terminate abruptly, and cause pain. All intermingle in the perpetual flow of events and continual transition of persons. All merge together and in time enlarge the inner awareness in its outward progress.

ADOLESCENT RELATIONSHIPS

In adolescence, human relationships take on a certain specific nature. A youth no longer reaches out towards others indiscriminately as people who may serve him or bring him bodily comfort. His perceptions have deepened and he recognizes well the different kinds of interpersonal relations. He wants to choose because his preferences are more numerous and his attractions and repulsions much stronger. There is always the group, and the adolescent must be a part of it. But there are also certain members of the group to whom he desires to relate more definitely.

Now-ness assumes a deeper intensity and the present moment is acutely vital. The urgency of youth creates spontaneity, freshness, eagerness, and a readiness for the plunge into reality. But the reality must be completely known before the plunge can be taken, lest all become meaningless and barren. A vigorous adventure into a pseudoworld may only turn the energies inward, where reality is avoided and the vitality of youth is squandered within the narrow limits of dreams and delusions.

What is this reality and how is it known? It is all that exists outside the self; everything as it really exists in the pure light of truth, in its own essence, its own nature. Reality is each being, each person, each thing, considered in its totality for itself, and then in its relationship to others. Reality refers to situations and circumstances, as well as to persons and things. Reality includes situations unclouded by faulty insight, or uncolored by exaggerated emotions, but understood as they exist in real surroundings; this time, this space, these conditions are actualities.

Reality is known best with full attention and comprehension. Existentially, reality is known in relation to the self. Reality is perceived in its entirety through ideas and perceptions, neither by the one nor the other alone. Dynamic responses are real in their own sphere, but belong to the knower in his affective life, rather than to the thing or situation perceived. Reality is not severed from dynamic functions. But because of their essence, dynamic functions are energies which *activate* but do not "know"; they have another mode of existence.

Objective reality surrounds us and is in us, for there are certain aspects that lie outside of our innermost subjectivity and are objective to intellectual or self-directive activities. Each individual must also know the reality that lies within himself, and the different modes of functions that are exterior and interior to himself. To know this reality may be the most difficult task of all, the hardest to manipulate, the most obscure to penetrate; yet the inner self is also a reality to be known, understood in its true, unique nature as a particular individuated being. Knowledge of external reality then will be enhanced by a comprehensive understanding of the inner reality, the true self.

ADOLESCENT GROUPS

Youth knows the group and seeks to integrate with it, to be entirely one with this living, pulsating, expression of togetherness. He moves within it as a part of its consciousness; his ideas, feelings, impulses, merge with the group and at times he does not distinguish his own from those of the group. He cannot separate himself from the group because he, in a sense, is the group and the group is himself. A powerfull oneness embraces the group and all that it stands for. It is many in one and one in many, reenforcing itself by many exchanges, but more so by the immersion of each individuality in the rhythm of its movement. The swing and sway of feelings in unison, of blended efforts smooths the edges of differences, and the group wends its way through many diverse courses. The presence of the group is felt everywhere; at home, in school, at church, and in the neighborhood. The course of the group may move toward achievement or destruction, and the tempo rises from the inner core which sets the pace, takes the lead, and initiates the projects.

The group process is complex, and participation may be direct or through related and remote channels. But always, the youth, even though he may live apart physically from others, seeks the group expression and in so doing realizes *himself* more intensely. The *group* is the adolescent's *world*; through it, his ideas develop and his judgments sharpen. Within this framework he reaches, step by step, for maturity. Without it he is deprived of an essential process in his own becoming. It is within the group that the adolescent best comprehends the range of feelings and emotions that permeate his being. He recognizes himself in others and in the group he realizes and exteriorizes the whole gamut of dynamic energies that dominate his living. He sees in his companions what he feels within himself.

In the group he can objectify what lies deep within, bring it into focus, lift it to consciousness so that he can know and choose. What lies within is often unknown, and what is unknown cannot be molded or drawn into creative realms. The realization of all this inner power brings the youth to the fullness of the person he strives to be. For each individual has inner resources and outer channels, and between the two a synchronized union fashions a wholeness that becomes action, effective, fruitful, renovating. Feelings are always feelings, and remain within the self, but generate an energy that moves outward. It is through these outward signs, gestures and actions, that feelings are expressed, but all these remain expressions only, and the true nature is always within. What another sees, estimates, or measures in the domain of feeling is merely the expression, the sign or the symbol, never the actuality itself. A quality of an object cannot be identified with the object, nor can an expression be identified with its source. There is always a certain interim, distance, or gap that lies between the source and its expression.

COMMUNICATION—AN ART

Perhaps much of the feeling as it exists internally may be lost in the media of communication. This is its natural course, yet the media may change it. Often the person himself may improve and refine the media so that the outward expression is a truer representation of his innermost self. Like the artist who may choose to use oil or water, wood or stone, to portray his ideas to others, so the person may choose many different media to relate his feelings and energies to those around him. It is the refinement of expression that becomes the art of communication. The effective communication of self in human relationships is far more complex than through art, poetry, or music.

Another great difference between the art of communication

through immediate self-expression and the arts of poetry, painting, and music is the difference in awareness. The painter knows well that paints are his only media, so he takes much care to choose well, to assimilate with a delicacy that befits the nobility of his thought. But when a man chooses to relate to another he is not always comparably aware of the fact that his medium is so important, that his feelings, his ideas, his inner world may be quickly understood by himself, but not so quickly grasped by others. He may forget that the effectiveness of his expressed self will depend on his mode of communication, the particular medium he chooses, and the pattern he gives it. More than this, he must know well the receptive mood of the one to whom he relates. A whole network of otherness lies before him, and to enter into these realms he must comprehend the systems and structures that are general to all and the more intricate interlacings which compose this other person in particular.

Nonverbal Communication

In childhood a person gingerly explores these strange and new approaches. Whatever brings success is soon repeated and assimilated. Habits are formed, grown, and strengthened, and many additional methods are rooted in the attempts to express the self. The routine activities a person performs day by day in the usual round of living may be far removed from his inner self. The functions all men have in common, such as eating, drinking, talking, sleeping, form a certain link of communal kinship but reveal only the most elementary likenesses. But even at best a category is limited, hemmed in, rigid and confining, and only when one transcends this category as an individual creative being does he do justice to himself. Even through these common ordinary activities that a person shares with all, he reveals something of his inner self.

The paradox is that he often consciously reveals what he wants to hide or what he does not know: his hostility, his fears, his resentments, his hopes. Throughout his growth, many habits have formed and have become a fixed part of his external relating. Perhaps he does not know or want these feelings to exist, and perhaps these unconscious attitudes even interfere with his knowing another; nevertheless, they are a part of this outward structure. The inner sources of the outward structure may change. The anger, fear, resentment, or hope may pass; what now may remain are the habits that arose from these feelings when they held sway. It is important to realize that outward habits, this residue of internal resistance, strife, or pursuit may create barriers that outlive the reality of the feelings themselves. The most common of exterior activities can include certain residual aspects. The impatient movements at table, the demands for quick service, the hasty grasp of a cup, the hurried thrust of a plate to another; all can convey a discordant atmosphere, a lack of congeniality. These actions may be habits, long removed from the initial sources, but the effects on others will be much the same. Only a person with deeper insight perceives beyond the surface and knows whether these minutiae are the remains of pressures long past or due to present stress.

LEVELS OF COMMUNICATION

But these gestures, and myriads of others, are not always the vestiges of bygone movements; they may be the immediate marks of the here and now. Whatever is their significance, their role in communications bears import. The impression on others is considerable. And this is but one meager example, a small glimpse into one particular common human function. The average day is filled with others: talking, walking, eating, drinking, working, regarding. But no matter how simple the activities performed in this exteriorized way, in the midst of others they are communicative. For the most part, these externals are of small consequence when we consider that, for the majority, these activities continue in vast surroundings, large groups, unheeded by most. But in the intimate, closed circles of small groups, of families, or between two people, these common functions become accentuated and assume a real aura of communication. It is inescapable.

To be with another, or with a few, is to communicate on a different level; communication takes on more dimensions and a deeper significance. In large groups we extend ourselves very differently than we do with one, two, or three. This difference is due not merely to the self but also the circumstances. The smaller the group, the deeper the self-extension, either voluntary or involuntary. In other words, when I am with one person, or a few persons, I will, by these very surroundings, communicate myself *more* than if I am with the same persons in a large group. Circumstances of closeness are themselves a kind of communication, and within this realm the person is known differently than in wider surroundings. But if in these same circumstances of closeness one also chooses to communicate himself, he will do so more readily. What is within will more easily be given to those with whom he shares a very simple but meaningful state of being.

ADULT COMMUNICATION

Some will say, "He is at his best with a crowd or in front of a large group." This may be true. He may be at his best to communicate a message, as an intermediary, but is this really communicating himself as he *is*? A good salesman gives a fine account of the quality of his commodities and convinces the listener of the values that his product possesses. Something of himself is inseparable from his salesmanship, but he may or may not have faith in the goods that he sells. In this case he exercises the skill of selling, which involves a certain coordination of his external powers. He communicates effectively for his merchandise, but not for himself. In commerce this kind of communication is important. In the exchange of things, what is personal is secondary or of no importance. Commerce is essentially a manipulation of things, of objects, so that successful salesmanship will in the end be gauged by the products sold, by quantities and not by any measure of personal growth. Again we see a type of relating that exists between persons but which is not truly personal and still far removed from encounter. The salesman does not relate with his whole being, but merely with an aspect of himself, predominately exteriorized.

There are other realms of activity that include relating.

These relationships differ in degree. Other metiers include relating to others, not for the exchange of objects external to both, but for purposes more directly concerned with the inward being of each. We notice this in such occupations as nursing, medicine, social work, and teaching. Even these vary considerably in themselves, especially when we consider their primary emphasis. Each will argue that he must be concerned with the whole man and in a certain sense this is true. We can never tear the human person asunder. He is always an undivided self. But there is also a possible emphasis of direction, a concentration on one or another aspect of his being.

Therefore, when we consider all from this viewpoint, we recognize different depths of relating. The doctor and the nurse, by their profession, seek primarily to care for the bodily health of their patient. They cannot ignore other propensities, such as attitudes or emotional life, for all are closely interwoven within him. However, they must first of all concentrate on his physical health and be concerned more immediately with his bodily needs. Through these interests they may easily enter into other channels of relating, but these will always be functions secondary to the purpose of medicine.

The social worker is similarly employed. He is working directly with people but his chief solicitude and responsibility is to provide for their enviornmental needs, to see that food, clothes, and shelter are sufficient. In order to accomplish this task successfully, the social worker must also relate to his clients with personal affability. Otherwise he will not be able to understand the extent of their needs and whether or not their social milieu will suffice for their growth.

Effective communication of a more personal kind is even more necessary in this position than it would be in the case of a salesman. There are some social workers who would make better salesmen, because they are highly successful in acquiring and disposing of funds and other things for people, but less capable of working with individuals personally for their own individual welfare. And there are probably many salesmen who would be better social workers because they often have little interest in their commodities and more interest in their clientele as persons. This is a moot question, but the significance here is simply to indicate the different kinds and levels of human communication.

Because of its specific purpose, teaching remains one of the most complex forms of communication, and also one of the greatest of human responsibilities. The mission of the teacher is to communicate truth, and his medium is always through ideas embodied in words, written or spoken. To communicate truth he must first know it himself, clearly and fully. There are some professors who lecture for hours without communicating ideas. The art of communication reaches a certain height in teaching because the demands are great and consequences immeasurable. No matter how simple the truth may be, the art of communicating it will demand great skill. The world of ideas is a subjective world and the teacher is obliged to convey his own ideas to the subjective world of his students. His skill as a teacher will often depend on his ability to grasp the differences existing between truth as it is in reality, and his own dynamic feelings toward this truth. Knowledge is positive; knowing is possessing; to teach is to give; truth is love possessed; communicating is giving; sharing a truth is loving.

Thus we see that teaching is the art of communicating truth, and in its own right is a powerful kind of relating. Through the teaching process, persons are often led to encounter. The nature of encounter is a more comprehensive kind of relatedness and of communication, but many constituents basic to teaching are likewise necessary for encounter.

Chapter 6

PERSONALITY AND IDENTITY

The professional counselor is approached by individuals with personal tensions that range from those of a normal person in distress to those of a person who is mentally ill. Mental illness itself includes many different levels and types of disturbances: neuroses, psychoses, psychopathologies, and other disorders that may have more definite physical causes. A basic requisite for any counselor is the awareness of his skills and expertise and also of his limitations. Some clients need a specialized clinician, others, a spiritual adviser; others, a counselor trained to assist normal persons with acute emotional upsets. Whatever their speciality, all counselors must be aware of the symptoms of personality problems as they are manifested from childhood to adulthood. Meaningful counseling occurs when a counselor is and feels competent to assist a client, or when he is knowledgeable enough to refer a client to a specialist trained to treat certain kinds of disorders. The skilled counselor, then, is expected to know when to counsel and when to refer a client to experts. An insightful comprehension of the nature of identity and its relationship to wholesome personality is a must for all counselors. Likewise, an awareness of the different types of personality problems and corresponding symptoms and manifestations is basic to effective counseling.

DEVELOPMENTAL ASPECTS OF IDENTITY

Early Beginnings

One day the toddler leaves his playpen, stumbles toward the mirror on the wall and with a shriek of exhilaration plasters his hand on its surface and cries: "Me." The first expression of self-awareness has emerged from within; and hereafter the infant passes through many further stages of self-recognition. He lives constantly in the world of things, and in the early beginning treats them all much alike. Powers of discrimination develop and he separates blocks from beads; he distinguishes sizes and shapes, sights and sounds. Along with these he identifies certain things more definite within himself and clings tenaciously to what is "his"; a bottle, a blanket, a teddy bear. These are for him, not for others. These are parts of himself, and when he shares them for a moment, he shares himself. Wherever he goes, these self-identities must accompany him, and he clutches onto them with all his might.

Later, his choices are even more intriguing and for a period of time he *becomes* something else in order to realize fully the inner delights he experiences. He plays no role when he attacks his preoccupied mother with a sudden thrust around her legs and says with a growl, "I am a bear." The lines of demarcation between his imaginary world and his perceptual life are very fluid and easily replace each other. His world often includes images that have such clarity that he has difficulty in distinguishing between them and the real objects. Sometimes a vivid dream confuses him and the world becomes topsy-turvy. Since he passes most of his waking hours on the floor, or in a playroom, removed from the adult world which towers above him, he concocts his own land, peopled by interesting fantasies that please him. His imagery grows, and daily he explores everything around him with all of his senses. Though he pays little direct attention to others, their presence is vital to his progress. Left to his mother or another familiar person he can remain for hours happily engrossed in his play.

The necessity of another's presence for the small child, apparently unmindful of his surroundings, is symbolic of every human being's need for the presence of another. It is one of the deepest of our subjective needs. The anguish of estrangement accompanies our existence and is frequently experienced throuhout life; its acuteness cannot be endured for too long without some disintegrating effects. The child with intuitive alacrity senses his aloneness at the moment his mother leaves him and he cries out in complaint. If he is overwhelmed by frequent estrangements, he recoils into himself and becomes silent. In the normal setting of supportive love and continual presence of another, the child develops rapidly and in his growth develops a distinction between his imagery and the objects he perceives.

Identity and the Older Child

The older child would feel ridiculous in saying, "I am a bear," but continues the game with "Let's pretend we are bears." The identity factor is stronger. The child now knows his name, his address, the family to which he belongs, his school, his church, his neighbors, and his country. And he identifies deeply with all of them. He also realizes himself more realistically and, in general, perceives, though not completely, the difference between his imagination and his experiences in reality. For in times of emotional stress, he, too, like his younger brother, tends to confuse what he sees objectively with what he imagines. In states of heightened emotion, he exaggerates sizes, numbers, and circumstances. After witnessing a fire, he may tell his playmates that there were ten fire engines when actually there were only five; or that there were 500 people watching when there were about 100. His inaccuracies are partly due to the mixture of imagination with his perceptions and partly due to the fact that his concepts are often vague and fragmented.

The older child builds his identity on many foundations and the solidity of these early beginnings influences him throughout his life. He identifies closely with his parents, and if circumstances interfere with this normal identification, his inner fiber is already weakened. He needs this firm association with his parents and family in order to gain the ground he requires for stability. When his parents are weak figures or are fearful and threatening influences in his life, he looks elsewhere for models from whom he can draw assurance. In his estrangement he may find solace in undesirable sources and these, in turn, will lead him to follow a deviant course in his personal growth. He depends almost entirely on his parents and other adult influences for the early formation of his sense of identity.

The older child also identifies with heroes, men who are esteemed as great successes, courageous, physically superior, supermen. The healthy child looks upward and outward for the ideals he hopes to attain. He attempts to absorb these figures immediately into his being with wholeheartedness. He dresses in cowboy clothes, proudly parades around in a spaceman's suit, and displays a wide variety of tokens to signalize his allegiance to certain individuals and groups. From all of these he draws something for himself, and since his media are still composed of *things*, these objects of identification take on singular importance in his life. With time, he grows tired of some but retains a certain affinity for his old associations. Something of them always remains within him. The stories of courage, of manliness, of daring adventure which he reads leave certain indelible marks on him and become interwoven into the self which uniquely assesses and incorporates all that is known.

Associations with others at school and joint activities in games grow in meaningfulness. The admiration received from peers becomes a prize that is avidly sought. Some children derive satisfaction in leading their playmates, others in following, but regardless of their position in the group, acceptance as an esteemed member becomes a primary goal. Much of what is absorbed is a mixture of the group ideal and the influences that form strong adult sources. Conflicts arise among these sources and the child usually solves them on a pragmatic basis. The child's criterion is usefulness, because he relates best to *things*. He evaluates on the basis of what is immediately useful for him in the achievements he presently seeks. Remotely, and with the assistance of adults who love him, he begins to see values for the future, but his own identity is too shaky to deal directly with intangibles. He is dominated by the concrete. He can grapple with it and he can comprehend it. His powers of knowing are primitive and his ideas and concepts are comparatively restricted in their application.

Who Am I?

The child's identity is increased particularly through immediate association and imitation, because his capacity to judge and to reason are minimal. The adolescent outgrows these limitations and it is precisely by rejecting them that he seeks to gain identity. Even though his parents may be, in reality, stable sources of identity, every adolescent at some period of his becoming looks at his parents with a skeptical eye and questions their sincerity and their principles with a forceful incredulity.

Parents, taken off guard, are often disturbed and irritated by the sudden taunts and criticisms hurled at them by their young assailants. Reason, logical or illogical, is the adolescent's favorite weapon for investigating his environment and he uses it relentlessly. He wants to know for sure if everything his parents do and say is really true, and if all adults are actually what they say or pretend to be. He must try out his world of reality, see if it can withstand the tests of reason. This is his search for identity. In his eagerness for independence and liberty from the protection of his parents he must be sure of himself before he can venture forth alone and sever the bonds which tie him to his dependency.

Paradoxically, throughout this entire period of struggle, and more than ever before, he requires the understanding, love, support, and reassurance of his parents. His inner stresses are severe, and the turbulence surrounding him is the growth process struggling for complete severance from the props it has known for so long.

The formation of identity for each person takes on a definite cast during adolescence. If identity does not move toward adult proportions within this period, it remains impoverished for a long time. Adolescence is the moment when the individual's self-extension crystallizes into a distinct personality pattern of its own. The vestiges of imitation, the outcomes of reasonings and comparisons, plus the adolescent's own choices, mold into a unity of subjective knowing and feeling and become the core identity of his being. His personality is the external relatedness that results from this inner formation. Two worlds, subjective and objective, merge into a harmony of thought and action. This unity leads to self-knowledge, self-awareness, self-acceptance and, above all, to self-direction.

This is "Who I am"—this person, in its uniqueness, its particular individuality, independent of another's thoughts or concepts—perhaps different from what is expressed to others—but this is the self, the authentic self, with no facades or pretensions. In the light of objectivity and subjective reflection, in this true knowledge there is security and strength, no matter how great the distance may be between the previous expectations and the actual existing self. The adolescent rests secure, without the threatening upset that comes from the endeavor to be something that he is not, without the fear that a constructed exterior could crumble into nothingness. This is freedom from the self-destruction that eliminates the "I" and leaves remaining only the pieces of a totally different self. This is the terror of the lack of identity, terror of the unknown, of the face behind the mask which may turn out to be grotesque and not the radiant creature imagined. This is the distressful, painful course of the adolescent, and more poignantly, the state of the anxiety-ridden neurotic or delusional psychotic who doesn't know who he is and becomes confused and lost in the search.

THE NEED FOR SELF-IDENTITY

The sense of identity differs from one person to another. Since identity is the core of personality, it is essential for effective social relationships. It is the stamina that provides the ability and the power to risk encounter. The greater the strength of identity the more potential for real encounter. The growth of identity is gradual and reaches a certain stature at each successive level. Certain augmentations correspond to social needs in each age group and must occur before the individual can face

his limitations and realize his true identity. With this full awareness of self the person arrives at a belief in himself. The continued growth of being and becoming is a strengthening and reaf-
firmation of the person underlying the personality.

Identity is firmly rooted in the person in his self-awareness
and enables him to know, to feel, and to behave in beneficial
ways: to communicate with others and to give of himself to
them, with or without return, to face the danger of risks, and to
make commitments. All of these modes of outward relating in
harmony with his own inner knowing and feeling is his unique
personality. It is a reality because he is a real person. It inheres
in him, but in so doing, does not lose its meaning, because whatever is personality is this person as subject, outwardly mani-
festing himself in his genuineness to others. The person himself
in his own reality is more than his personality, since he is more
than his relatedness. He is first of all a being, *this* being, and
through his personality, he shares the uniqueness of his being
with others, but ever remains the unified self. The person as this
self retains an incommunicable identity which transcends his
personality. He can give of himself, but he cannot give his being-
ness to another. Through his personality he can extend himself,
but he cannot relinquish his identity. Identity maintains an indestructible reality of its own. Even a loss of the sense of identity
does not dissolve the identity of this individual person. A loss of
a sense of identity causes confusion and may involve amnesia,
disorientation, and other mental disabilities; but even when the
person is unable to recall his name, or is deluded and thinks he is
another, he still remains this one distinct person.

DIMENSIONS OF PERSONALITY

The quality of personality usually designated as attractive,
personable, likable, or appealing, arises from a combination of
strong identity, genuine self-awareness, and openness to others.
The unique combination of these internal attributes will vary
with each individual and give rise to unique expressions. The
degree of personableness will have some bearing on the developmental stages of identity during childhood and adolescence.

The amount of freedom a child has had in being himself rather than a product of what his parents wanted him to be, or made him be, will be a determining factor in the firmness of his identity and the consequent attractiveness of his personality.

Potentially, every person is attractive and is capable of being generally personable and likable. He does not become so by "acquiring" certain traits, or by striving to imitate this person or that. In the very attempts to fabricate exterior characteristics, the person himself becomes less himself and less appealing to others, and the structure he builds becomes a barrier in his relation to others. There may be apparent improvements, and he may seem more successful in his interchange with others, but these acquired effects will be temporary. The true source of his attractiveness is his unique self, and he grows more personable for others as he becomes more truly himself. It is his effort to be, to be what he is, fully, without simulation, and to be genuine, that appeals to another. Attempts to imitate, to be other than what he really is, to assume false exteriors, make a person repellent to others. What does not belong to him as this particular person does not "fit," and a person is most attractive in his own becoming because his own reality and self-actualization are more befitting.

For example, all virtues are good in themselves and objects of our desires; but each person will become truly charitable, humble, merciful, tolerant in his own unique way. He cannot reconstruct himself or make himself into the other person by imitating him as a model, by being a replica; but he can *become* more charitable. A deep psychological difference lies between these two approaches. In fashioning certain codes of behavior in one's self that are founded on another's belief, another's system of values, one builds a composition of parts that can easily disintegrate. One cannot give or teach a value to another person, because value is not a content. But an individual can provide the means for another to exercise the act of valuing. In much the same way, a person cannot pick up or acquire values, but he can absorb them by experiencing them. If the patterns of behavior that I have formed do not arise from within me, then they are adjuncts and can be readily discarded. But what I become by the light of my own convictions and for my own motives is my own growth. This is myself in my becoming. Values are learned in a living situation and are effective only as they become internalized, grow within, and become my genuine authentic self.

Many persons play a role and act a part, but when there is no longer a stage or an audience, the role loses its significance and dissolves. There is no set pattern of externals that constitutes charity or humility. This person, truly loving, in extending himself to others is charitable; in being himself, is humble. We learn these virtues by knowing their essences, not their externals. We know their essences when we experience them in charitable and humble people, not by studying books or reading lists of characteristics. Even examples, verbally expressed, are of little consequence without an experience of them. Illustrations may help us to clarify our thoughts, to communicate verbally, but they are not the first sources of our knowing these qualities. As one experiences charity, he comes to know it and to understand its many facets, for love transcends descriptions, words, and expressions. A child learns to love only by being loved. He learns humility and genuineness only as he realizes it in action; and so on, through the whole range of virtues. Because it is easier to take the line of least resistance, he will also more quickly learn subterfuge, for it is often easier to hide behind a structure than to be real. At times it is easier to be angry than to love, and if a person has experienced more anger and hostility than love he will tend to be hostile. This is the process of growth and becoming in its most natural flux.

Positive Personality

An attractive personality, then, is this person extending his real self to others. Acquired rituals, patterns of speech, artificial exterior performances are not the ingredients of charm. These are artifacts and detract from the real self. Every culture contains diverse customs and conventions, and these are necessary for certain occasions but, as a person, one must distinguish between what is genuinely himself and what is merely conventional. For example, if one dines with people of India it may please them to eat rice with one's fingers; in another culture it may be more appropriate to use a fork. The habits and manners will differ from one milieu to another, and what is important for each person is that he knows what he himself is, apart from the many acquired externals. Each person will always be what he is, and wholesome growth and development will consist in the continued extension of the real self.

It is not the "perfect" person who is loving, humble, and attractive; in reality this image is a myth. It is the person who is real, true, and genuine who is capable of loving others, being himself for others, with all his limitations; this is the virtuous person and the attractive personality. There are many lovable people who have obvious faults, but whom we love and esteem. Their lovableness is greater than their defects. In order to be one's self and express that self to others, love must be greater than limitations. In the expansiveness of love, other shortcomings diminish; in the absence of love, they augment. The irresistibility of the child is his genuineness; he is so much his real, true self. The childish person, however, is not himself because his potentialities are hidden behind the characteristics of the child he once was, but is no longer. He is only partly what he potentially could be. He is selfish and unattractive. In his becoming, a true and genuine person relinquishes these childish habits and his ego enlarges, gains self-awareness, and he loves another for the sake of the other.

CULTURAL INFLUENCES

The crucial problem of our day is to live in a culture built on things, in a technological society revolving around things, and yet not become "things" ourselves, or regard others as things. The increase of maladjusted individuals and the large numbers of disintegrated personalities indicate the gravity of this problem. The most serious deficiency in our efforts to build a better world may possibly arise from the influences psychology itself has unconsciously absorbed from this society. Born in technology, psychology has served technology more than man himself. In its sincere efforts scientifically to discover the full nature of man, it has lost a part of his reality by borrowing too much from the scientific methods suitable for the investigation of *things*. A reevaluation of what a person really is in himself, and for himself, may help us to reorient to people as persons, rather than as mere objects of research.

For example, in personality studies we have viewed man as a structure, a gestalt, an operational model, as some assembly of parts. All of these approaches have been fruitful, up to a point. But as a result of these approaches, we know more about man in his exterior functioning than we know about him in his internal reality. When there is harmony between these two aspects we meet no great problem; but if a man's exterior behavior is not congruent with his inner knowing and feeling, he soon suffers some kind of disintegration which also affects his behavior. Our efforts to prevent this suffering or to alleviate it have not been as successful as our research on his behavior. We need a balancing program to investigate and know the inner man. We have more knowledge of facts than we can effectively use on behalf of the suffering individual. A productive machine cannot be a model for an effective person. A deeper penetration of man's sense of identity and of the inner man behind the outer structure, of this living, anguished person will lead us to new and different considerations.

For several decades, behaviorism has dominated the study of children and all phases of developmental psychology. We have all absorbed many attitudes from this method, and our focus has been on the behavior of the human person more than on the inward self beneath behavior. We know a great deal about man's external behavior, and it is now opportune to gain a glimpse into the interior realm, into the profundity of man's being-in-the-world. We cannot separate the two entirely or we lose the person, for the individual is a union of his interior experiences and his outward expressions.

A sense of identity, then, begins early and continues on throughout the life cycle. It forms the inner fiber of personality and is the integrating factor within; it weaves together our exterior behavior, our values, our motives. Values experienced as worthy and meaningful for the self, are internalized into becoming. We reorient and re-form ourselves. When exteriorizations have in themselves true meaning and are not mere functions routinely performed, then one can incorporate them. As long as exterior behavior is not significant to one as a person, he does not integrate it into his own being. He can only use it for a time, as long as it is useful, and then will discard it. Certain kinds of behavior are helpful tools and are meant to be such.

For example, in advertising, a businessman may realize that an appeal to customers that employs colorful banners with symbols increases sales more than the distribution of leaflets, so he discontinues the output of leaflets. An actor finds out that when he modulates his voice and uses a certain acquired accent for his part that he plays his role more dramatically. But when he is among his friends he no longer uses this accent. He doesn't need to play this role with them. They prefer him as Joe, rather than as Hamlet. In all of these cases, the activities or mannerisms are useful for a time, and when they no longer are helpful they are eliminated. None of them has become internalized or absorbed into the self.

VALUES

Many more important forms of behavior may be much the same for a person, and with little more significance. One may accumulate many habits consciously or unconsciously that never become integrated within. Whatever remain as adjuncts or aggregations of activities will have no permanent value for the person concerned. For example, an adolescent who has learned useful behavior patterns for obtaining indulgence from his parents, or favors from his friends, which have no personal meaning for him, will quickly substitute others when he no longer needs these ploys. An adolescent who has no other real values, but merely an accumulation of pragmatic rituals, is often unable to face the responsibilities of adulthood. He has not incorporated enough values and motives into his own being-ness to stand on his own feet. When he suddenly realizes that these patterns exist mechanically outside his real self and are not distinct properties of his own, he panics, and doubts the worth of himself and all his surroundings. As these experiences increase and he sees that he has identified with externals as his only security, he feels rudderless. To have an identity of his own, the adolescent must have values and motives of his own choice; values he esteems as significant for him as this person. He needs more than instruments for obtaining approval. Actions performed blindly, without comprehension of their purpose, rarely become meaningful for him. An approach-avoidance system is not sufficient for identity growth. The adolescent must know the good and the value of an action before he can freely embrace it. He cannot find value in the mere imitation of another's behavior. When the threat of punishment is removed, this conformity to another's code will vanish. Or, if he has acquired habits of behavior completely built on approval, these habits will soon become extinct when the approval is no longer present, or when it is no longer needed.

Identity must come into its own, and results from a process of valuing, esteeming, integrating, and not from a program of training. Behavior patterns clearly perceived as a means to an end may be integrated, providing the relationships between the means and the end is grasped. If an athlete realizes by himself that smoking impairs his speed and that it shortens his breath he will be more likely to sacrifice it than if it is a mere recommendation from the coach. If a student personally comprehends the worth of a subject he is studying, he will more likely learn it well. If it is simply something required for a certificate, he will retain very little of it as permanent knowledge. For the adult who sees in his job an opportunity for self-expression and the chance to be a person in the fullness of his being, this position will become an integral part of his whole living process.

The process of growth in identity is growth as a person, and this means that the system of values which forms the basis of behavior is a personal system and has meaning for the individual concerned. The integrated person with an identity of his own realizes and performs many actions that have no pragmatic value. The courage to be oneself requires many nonpragmatic assertions. Courage is also expressed in acts that appear useless to others, but which are personally esteemed as valuable. Strong identity requires courage to execute personal values and motives, regardless of resistance or criticism from others.

DEVELOPMENTAL VALUES

Even in childhood, the idea of valuing something for itself rather than purely for its pragmatic purpose must be introduced. This is difficult because the child naturally is utilitarian in his outlook. He can, at least, learn to esteem what is more worthwhile even though it may not be immediately useful; but he learns these deeper meanings only in an atmosphere of love. A child who lives amid contention and disputes, and who witnesses a daily display of hostility between his parents, who exists in fearful surroundings, cannot develop lofty motives or high ideals. He struggles to survive and to surmount his insecurity. His identity remains weak, because he is not sure of his evaluations. The inconsistencies he witnesses cause him frequently to shift his values and he tends to be insecure and unstable. Unless he has some unusual opportunities for recovery and wholesome compensation, his insecurity increases. In adolescence he identifies with a group for a while and if he somehow assimilates values from his other socializations, he may reach an identity that suffices, but he will suffer many inadequacies. Adolescents from this kind of environment hover between delinquency and acceptable social behavior. Their own convictions waver and they move with the strongest wind.

The child who perceives a real relationship between his parents that also includes himself can be led to see a few values that do not bring direct returns to himself. At times he experiences a yen for courage, and demonstrates surprising stamina when he must uphold a conviction. He will sacrifice small comforts like extra gadgets and toys when he realizes that the denial will be helpful to his parents. He voluntarily performs helpful chores around the house that require concentrated effort. Some children silently withhold their requests for clothes or desired objects if they understand that these possessions would be a financial strain on their parents. A boy will often go without a baseball mitt, not because he is afraid to ask for it, but because he does not want to burden his parents further. The child performs these sacrifices without resentment when his home is dominated by love. This kind of evaluation the child makes for himself is an inestimable strength in his own identity. He has witnessed the kind of sacrifice that is born of love, has intuitively sensed its value, and wants to embrace it as a part of himself.

The adolescent who has known love in his home life may also demonstrate a certain valor and praiseworthy generosity on behalf of his family or friends. Adolescents may endure a lot of fatigue and deprivation in order to work and pay their school expenses. They often do so without any demand or encouragement from their parents, simply for the purpose of being helpful. In the world of sports, adolescents can be heroic in their self-denial for the team and for many group enterprises. Adolescents equipped with a firm identity are more able to function on higher levels of motivation and are more able to evaluate without utilitarian purposes. Selfless love experienced over a long period of time is the prime source of a sense of identity; it is stabilizing, unifying, and vigorous. When the unerring eye of the child has perceived the sincere love of his parents and, as an adolescent, has intellectually scrutinized this parental love and found it valid, he is on the way to discovery of his own identity. He knows love and, in turn, he himself can love others. Less fortunate children must find substitutes or compensations or perhaps will be able, with the help of a good counselor, to mature sufficiently in order to establish an identity they can realize as their own.

GROWTH OF IDENTITY

The dispositions that foster identity in children are attitudes of regard for another person. The child is a being with his own individuality from the first moment of his existence. But the assurance of his own identity as a human being depends much on the circumstances of his early life; the identity an adolescent realizes is influenced somewhat by his childhood. An individual reaches a full sense of identity over the course of time, and he does so more through his experiences than through axioms. Only when a child experiences love does he grow secure. The overprotective mother who is minutely solicitous for her child's welfare because of her own insecurity or guilt feelings does not instill confidence in him. The child grows unstable in this atmosphere of a compensatory parent. The child who is showered with expensive gifts from parents, but who is frequently left behind with others for weekends or vacations suffers keen emotional deprivation. The child who never really possesses anything of his own because his parents only let him "use" his toys or his pocket money, or his clothes, does not differentiate much between his possessions and those of his parents. Consequently, he often abuses or destroys things around the house out of resentment towards his parents whom he identifies with his toys, clothes, and house property. This delinquency occurs when parents select his clothes, limit the use of his own possessions, and forbid his sharing with others. As a result, the child is retarded in his concepts of responsibility so closely allied to his identity.

DEPRIVATION

There are countless examples to describe circumstances that weaken the child's ego. His individuality increases only when he knows *felt-love*, and when he enjoys a special place in his home as a distinct member of the family. Disturbed children often reveal their feeling of loss and homelessness when they are deprived of these essential human relationships. In general, most cases of seriously disturbed mental patients can be traced to these deprivations in early ego-identity. A very vivid example of starvation in ego-growth is related by Lindner (1956) in describing one of his case studies. The psychotic patient, in speaking to the therapist, says, "I couldn't find out about myself from inside because she (his mother) got rid of me too fast. So I had to have things to tell me who I was and . . . I didn't even have that" (p. 26). Another small boy, who in his desperate struggle to maintain himself against many odds, fought his way through the neighborhood, in the classroom, on the playground, complained to his counselor: "I can't just let them think I'm nobody." In his own home his parents, preoccupied with marital disputes, sorely neglected him and he was left to fend for himself. Two little sibling girls, six and eight years old, had been shuttled around from place to place, suffered brutality and neglect and were finally left at an orphanage. In a routine meeting with a counselor some reference was made to one little girl about her family. She quickly pointed to the classroom where her sister was and said, "My family is in there." At least she had her sister with whom she could identify. Further problems in identity for adolescents arise in the confusion engulfing the younger generation who are obliged to live in a milieu based on meaningless ideals and models.

Children who are denied the normal emotional satisfactions are as pathetic as children who are physically undernourished. They are haunted by a hunger that is more acute and disabling. They become interiorly languid and inert and their ability to relate adequately to others is seriously impaired. The need for identity stems from one's existence and the drive for survival outstrips other energies for seeking satisfaction. One desperately strives to survive as a person. On this level he struggles not only to live but to be someone; he fights against non-being. His whole self contends against all the odds in order to be this person, this individual distinct from all others. In the midst of this combat the adolescent is very upset and frustrated if without sufficient certainty of his own personal identity he is obliged to leave his parents. His continued increase in self-awareness and self-consciousness also demands self-assurance; he must come to know well what this self really is, and he must become autonomous. The source of anxieties, anguish, and estrangement of the most disturbing kind arises from his fear of the unknown within himself; from the uncertainty of his own existence, nature, origin, his place in the world where he finds himself to be without initiative of his own. He cannot bear the thought of being anonymous, of being nothing. When he has arrived at a threshold that seems to point to his nothingness, his anxiety turns into despair.

The depersonalizing effects of our industrialized society are numerous, and the individual must orient himself to the pressures of his environment without being swallowed up by them. His happiness as a person and his effectiveness as a human being depends on his resistance to a powerful depersonalizing society. An overidentification with *things* is revealed in the sudden psychic traumas that sometimes occur when people have suffered a loss of property or of prestige. Many individuals cannot survive these losses psychologically. Their whole lives have been enmeshed in concern for their property that has usurped the place of human love. Or in their personal relationships they have never reached encounter, so that others who are loved are loved as objects. Misfortune in either of these cases results in despondency or a loss of identity. A personal love between two human individuals begins to deteriorate when both become more interested in sharing *things* than each other's presence. A marriage, for example, in which the relationship is based on the accumulation of property and money or on building up prestige and social status, rests on shifting sands and the dissolution of projects may easily lead to the breakup of the marriage. This is a marriage between two persons with weak personal identities, each trying to construct a strong self on the possession of things, and consequently their mutual exchange is reduced to a cooperative enterprise.

Identity Crises

For the young person, the struggle for identity is the most crucial of all the growing pains he endures; his future as a mature person depends on his success. The teenager's anguish of estrangement is unusually painful and he feels a complete stranger to himself, at times even feeling unfamiliar with his own body. Everything within him seems to change from moment to moment. His restlessness and constant need for diversion reflect the fluidity within him. He senses his proneness to influence and suggestibility, and waivers from one viewpoint to another. He does not want to identify with his family or parents, because it is from this root that he is endeavoring to break away. His inner uncertainties are the source of his perplexities and anxieties, and he finds his chief consolation in identity with his peer group. The lone-wolf adolescent moves toward the fringe of psychopathy and even suicide unless he finds a substitute in some other mature human person.

Counselors know many examples of students who are overcome by aloneness and who feel crushed by estrangement. A young boy reared in a superior economic stratum, who had all the comforts of life except the warmth of parental affection, cried out in despair, "I feel I have no middle, as if I had no insides at all." He had been raised by parents who overrated social graces and formalities; his motivations for conformity were mostly based on obtaining parental approval. In order to secure their attention, he spent most of his time in gaining prestige: by dressing well, by meticulous manners and courtesy. In college, away from the immediate domination of his parents and in a setting where these externals did not guarantee approval, he became unusually sloppy, vulgar, and abusive. Once the reins were dropped he went to the other extreme and was ostracised by his companions. He knew no middle course, no real self-control, no internalized standards of his own. His behavior patterns had been built on the approval of his parents and held no real meaning for him.

The frequent taunts heard among teenagers themselves reveal their sensitivity and awareness of pseudoidentification: "Who do you think you are, the King of Siam?" or "He thinks he's Superman." In one case history, a young college girl whose parents had both remarried, leaving her stranded in the middle, demonstrates the proportions that loneliness can reach when identity is weak. In her freshman year of college she arrived at the beginning of the semester to find that she had been placed in the new residence hall; in this particular dormitory all the rooms were singles. In a state of panic she ran down the hall and out the door directly to the counselor and trembling with terror exclaimed: "I can't stay in that room for one moment, not for one single moment." On opening the door and seeing the single accommodations, her sense of loss was so acute she could not even enter the room, but fled the building as if she had seen a monster. Her need for companionship was so great and her ability to relate well to others so inadequate, that she could not face life at college without an assigned partner who would at least have to share the room with her.

Karen Horney, Harry Stack Sullivan, and others have referred to various types of human relations to determine the states of mental illness as compared to those of mental health. These descriptions realistically portray the problems of neurosis and psychosis. Whatever else these states are, they are always impairments in human relatedness. Mentally ill people cannot function as human persons because they cannot relate to others effectively, or they relate on a minimal level rather than on a maximal level. They have the capacity to relate but the inability to exercise it. Internal dynamic patterns are the chief barriers to the relatedness required for normal human functioning.

Physical conditions such as brain damage, tumors, cerebral deteriorations, and other kinds of pathological disturbances may also be causes of disturbed relationships. In the case of mental defectives there is also a physical cause for disturbed inter-personal relationships. The mental defectives will always be confined to certain deficiencies because of limited capacities. Patients suffering from brain damage and other cerebral pathologies may or may not recover their full capacity. Medical and psychological research during the past decades have indicated that the most numerous disorders are those without any apparent physical pathology. In most of these cases, impairment of human functioning arises from other sources.

Chapter 7

MENTAL ILLNESS

Clinicians find it increasingly difficult to distinguish clear-cut types of mental disorders and are more hesitant to diagnose maladies by classic categories. These new observations also indicate the advances made by clinicians themselves who have more skillfully penetrated the worlds of mentally disturbed patients and gained more awareness of the inner complexities of the mentally ill person. The comprehension of relationships between syndromes and inner patterns of thought and feeling has improved considerably. Yet, with all of these advances and observations, the number of mental disorders mounts steadily and the problem of treatment and cure is acute. Prevention is the best answer, and for this approach we need a more complete knowledge of personality itself, and of the basic potentials that enable a person to establish good interpersonal relationships.

We have designated personality as the capacity of the human person to relate to others effectively. Disturbances in personality will involve some impairment or derangement in a person's communication and relatedness to others. From this viewpoint we can observe the problems, the obstacles, and the systems of habits that may account for confused states originating in inadequate interpersonal relationships. One person is mentally disturbed because he relates in a bizarre fashion, or he seems incapable of relating sufficiently to maintain himself independently. Another person may be able to relate to others, but unsatisfactorily, and in ways that continually render him agitated or anxious. Without oversimplification, since the network of interchange is limitless, mental disorders will be best understood in terms of disturbances in effective human relationships. A consideration of particular kinds and patterns of relating that cause mental illness will indicate how the personality disintegrates.

PROBLEMS IN RELATIONSHIPS

A mentally disturbed person suffers in his human relationships. This is always a part of his problem, no matter what particular bizarre syndrome he may have acquired. At the very base of his illness lies his inability to have and maintain social interchange with others. The human person, essentially social in nature, and who because of physical or functional impediments is unable to know, enjoy, and exchange with others, becomes mentally disordered. The study of personality and of personality disorders from this frame of reference will differ decidedly in emphasis from an investigation which examines behavior in terms of traits, characteristics, and categories. The latter approach will look for entities, for contents, measurement. Personality considered as the capacity and power of the person for relating, rather than as a aggregate or sum of traits, will approach the study of mental illness in another way.

Personality is more concerned with the flow of human communication, the movement and direction of human relationships, the interweaving of powerful dynamic energies, the increase of vitality, the forwardness of creativity. These changes may be more difficult to know and observe and will be much harder to measure and describe; but they may also indicate more clearly the direction necessary for development, for removal of impediments, and for relief from distress. If the anguished and suffering person benefits more from this approach than the statistician does, it is the one which must be chosen. Certain classifications have been valuable and have given clinicians and investigators something to hold on to. They have benefited scholars and students, and have accomplished a purpose. But a better knowledge of human relationships, nebulous and intangible though this may seem to be, will bring us closer to the subjective world of the mentally ill. These individuals profit little from being in this category or that. What alleviates their pain is human warmth known and received with the hope of some felt enlightenment, some experienced joy, which will gradually enable them to move forward out of their self-imprisonment into a receptive world of otherness.

In an attempt to observe the basic ways of relating we may make the following observations: A person may give to others but not receive, or may receive from others and not give, or neither give nor receive, or he may give and receive. As we consider each of these relationships or directions of human energies from one to the other, we realize the extent and variance of differences that qualify any and all of these movements. In each of these ways the self relates in a greater or lesser degree. And the extension of self, the manner and intensity of the exterior expression, or the lack of it, will be at the basis of either mental health or mental illness.

To supplement the deficiencies and to provide a setting wherein the impediments in relating may be diminished, the clinician or counselor will gain insight by understanding the different levels and modes involved in these basic human directions. For example, if the schizophrene is approached as a person who seems incapable of either giving or receiving, rather than a person who is hebephrenic, paranoic, or catatonic, he will be better understood in terms of how he relates. Regression and withdrawal also indicate movement of energy and better describe the schizophrene than other more definitive characteristics. However, the problem of the clinician will always be to provide a situation wherein the patient can grow sufficiently in order to relate effectively. This will be the basis of a therapy session.

In the major psychoses, the patient's ability to maintain human relationships is seriously impaired. He is unable to function in a normal setting, and treatment often requires hospitalization or segregation from others. The distance between his subjective operations and his external behavior is too great, or in his attempts to coordinate the two he separates himself from others.

SCHIZOPHRENIA

Undoubtedly there are many internalized experiences of the schizophrene which we do not know thoroughly. Some of the projective techniques have helped us to enter this world; but the most valuable of all will be whatever we can know of this world directly, such as: the therapist's way of relating, description of his successes, and the fragmented movements of the schizophrene himself toward a world from which he repeatedly recoils. The schizophrene may be described as a person who is unable to give or to receive. He has become walled up in his own ego, and slowly suffers from ego-starvation as he recedes more and more from relatedness.

Some phases of schizophrenia dramatize this encapsulated state. The schizophrene who becomes inert, apathetic, listless, is content to remain immobile physically, completely enclosed within his own inner domain. He may remain in this uncommunicative state for long periods of time. Therapeutic attempts to reach across the gap between him and the outer world meet many difficulties, and contacts are often very limited. The mental processes that eventually lead a person to schizophrenia are gradual but steady. As the normal person continually grows in his ego strength he moves outward toward others. In the case of the schizophrene, the direction has been inverted, and each stage of development has been an advance inward instead of outward. Problem situations were resolved by turning away from them, looking within to fantasy where these problems did not exist because they were refused entrance. Painful experiences suffered because of rejection, hostility, or exclusion were assuaged by daydreams. Fantasy provides the warmth of total acceptance and the glow of praise and esteem. In these subjective realms the world is friendly; encounter is not exchange but, rather, adoration absorbed.

In the aura of total subjectivity there is no "movement,"

but rather a fixed state of inertia, a pool where all remains submerged. The inner muteness is disturbed only by attempts from the outside to break through the protective guards. The stillness is neither happy nor sad, but empty and complacent. For the schizophrene, outside this inner world lie dangers, pitfalls, threats, and pain.

Withdrawal Tendencies

The deeper the withdrawal, the further removed the schizophrene feels from the menace of foes, antagonistic forces. Pain and agony occur when glimpses of the exterior world penetrate the awareness. For the schizophrene, outside contacts may be traps which seek to capture him in his continued flight from reality. Communication is a danger which may destroy the bulwark of resistance and bring in messages that disturb the voiceless and painless void surrounding him. The ego is too weak to give and too fearful to receive. The inner world is safer and less agonizing.

This extreme withdrawal of the long-term schizophrene is a result of many lesser habits converged into a total removal of the self from others. The infant lies in his crib unable to give of himself and, in a sense, unable to receive as a person; but he absorbs all that comes to him and, in so doing, grows physically and psychologically. The schizophrene often resembles the infant in this state of absorption, except that the absorption is more mental than physical. But the comparison helps to realize the subjective state of the schizophrenic person.

Not all schizophrenics, of course, regress to this degree; many are able to recover through therapeutic means, and begin the slow process of moving toward the outer world. The ego must grow and evolve before any definite approach to others can be made. The beginnings of communication are symbolic, and the schizophrenic person, especially, depends on the use of signs to venture into relationships with others. For many disturbed patients, symbols are the media of communication and the schizophrenic's symbols have a particular quality of their own. For the therapist, the signs and symbols become valuable means of entrance to the interior world of the patient. Some externalizations, such as grimacing or manual gesticulations are fairly common, but the uniqueness of each patient introduces signs particular to him. For example, the use or avoidance of colors which have specific meaning for this patient may be related to his basic conflict.

Certain sounds symbolize bells, trains, sirens, or other objects and situations that have some bearing on the inner struggle. Entering into this whole new realm and network of meaning, the therapist may be able to comprehend the patterns of movement which push away from conflict, and he will also gain more insight into the nature of the conflict itself. More likely, the core conflict, as it exists in the psyche of the patient, will not be understood by the therapist until he has realized the dynamic patterns developed over a period of time. In a disturbance resulting from the inversion of evolvement, the methods of approach will often follow a similar path, i.e., moving from an awareness of what these particular signs—gestures, grimaces, colors, sounds, smells—indicate, through other concentric divisions and finally to the conflict itself as it is perceived by the client. In this inner domain there will lie some fundamental problems of human relatedness. There will be many complexities arising from the particular situation of the patient; but there will also be schizophrenic complexities, movements of shrinking away from some painful relationship with others, retreating in order to avoid further anguish.

Regressions

Many of the movements of the schizophrenic are comparable to those that belong to earlier stages of human development. And by recalling the way in which a child reacts, we can gain some insight into schizophrenic patterns. The latter will be much more complex in their origins, but comparable in expression. The infant is helpless and of himself can make no approaches to others, or only do so by some feeble gesture of an instinctive nature. This helplessness and inability to meet another may cause many to overlook him, excepting those who love him.

The severely regressed schizophrene is much the same. He has returned to an infantile stage and of himself is unable to make contacts. Similarly, he may be overlooked or ignored because his resistance is silent. Isolation from others will arrest his growth, and tend to solidify this infantile pattern. Like the child, he needs to be surrounded by others even though he seems unaware of them and is unable to initiate communication. His inward movements will not change without the presence of others. The immature self of the schizophrene can neither give nor receive of itself, but may be drawn from his retreat by warmth, presence, and other methods comparable to the approach toward infants and young children. Like the infant, he is completely egotistical and, because of his psychic barriers, absorbs but does not receive. His intake needs to be infused.

General Patterns

Schizophrenic persons who are less withdrawn use certain media for communication. They move through things in a world of things. They fabricate delusions and communicate through them, give and receive through delusionary resources. Whatever fantasies serve to substitute best for their need become woven into speech mannerisms and gesticulations. Just as one can communicate to a child best through stories or through toys, so one can communicate best with the schizophrene through his delusionary preoccupations. To break a child's toys is to destroy his universe. In much the same fashion one can demolish the props of the schizophrene if his delusions are removed prematurely. He most outgrow his delusions. For a child, growth seems to pass quickly because it is a natural enfolding; for the schizophrene, the process may seem to be prolonged because his physical growth is completed. Self-growth requires time and involves multiple factors. In the case of the schizophrene, the body developed while the self was arrested at some level or other. Whatever will bring the self to maturity will be whatever provides it with the chance to become. Self-growth requires time and the skillfull assistance of a therapist.

Recent observations seem to indicate that schizophrenic pa-

tients in our times exhibit more generalized patterns than patients of around the 1960s. External manifestations are often
less distinct, and the distance between the schizophrenic himself
and the outside world apparently is not so great. In other words,
many schizophrenic patients show ego immaturity in their ability
to communicate on deeper, mature levels, but exteriorly are able
to perform simple functions of communication. They walk
around, talk more in limited groups and, in general, display
fewer bizarre activities. However, the inability to give of themselves and to receive, in the less tangible but more essential ways,
are just as evident and serious.

For example, a young schizophrenic housewife may speak
with others, sometimes lucidly, at other times in a very *unreasonable*, but still not *startling* manner. But her care of the children is
erratic, her ability to give them warmth is nil, and she may ignore them in ways that are dangerous for them. Sometimes her
illness is revealed not in dramatic or strange behavior but in her
absurd, unstable, and seriously fluctuating relatedness to others.
At one moment she may play with her children and the next moment neglect to feed them. She may appear to do the chores
around the house, but may be careless about burning things,
may forget essentials, and thus endanger the children or others
with whom she lives.

New approaches in therapy have met these changes by providing patients with more opportunities to be in groups, arrang-
ing more situations for mingling with others, even though the
patients are noncommittal or unresponsive. Isolation is avoided
if possible. The use of psychodrama and other techniques have
attempted to draw the patients outward, and to provide opportunities of expression.

Manic Depression

Depressed States

The manic-depressive in either phase of his cycle is moving
outward to the extreme, beyond the limits of normal extension.
He gives by imposing himself, by pushing his outwardness upon

others, by demanding entrance into all and every domain. His extreme aggression is especially noted in his manic stages, but even in the depressed states the psychic movement is outward. The depressed person is not *withdrawn*. He often resorts to prolonged periods of melancholy and silence; but his is not the taciturn state of the schizophrene. The depression is accusatory, either self-condemning or directed to others. His silence and melancholy are filled with censure, with guilt verdicts of many kinds. His brooding is not an inward spiraling but an outward denouncement. He is overwhelmed by his own self-condemnation, and his solitude and anguish are expressions of pleading, beseeching, bewailing the evils his fantasy embraces. The seriously depressed person is overconcerned with himself, and his whole exterior bristles with disapproval. Whether he displays manic symptoms or depressed symptoms, his basic conflict is one of self-defense. His line of action is protection rather than escape, and his time is spent in pushing away threats to his ego. In his depression his defenses are plaintive and mournful. He pours himself out, pushes himself to the outside, to others, to all, indiscriminately. Whether others are present or not makes little difference to the seriously depressed person because his outflow is without reasonable purpose, and not for others, but rather for himself. His giving is not a sharing, or with thought of another, but a disruptive function of his ego in self-defense.

The depressed patient is quite aware of his surroundings, and the anguish he suffers internally is comparable to the misery he shows. His fantasies are grotesque and threatening and completely out of proportion to reality. He endures many mental tortures because of the imagery that preoccupies him and leads him to despair. His internal life is plagued with upheavals and turmoil and his thoughts are permeated by devastating feelings of culpability, failure, error, and sin. Unable to endure the intensity or to contain the endless motion of his own thoughts, he plunges himself into a state of depression as a measure of vindication.

The monologues of the depressed person consist of endless repetitions of transgressions committed, real or imagined. He mourns outwardly and continuously because of his failures. He grossly exaggerates his misdemeanors and enumerates his faults

in detail over and over again. Misdeeds are multiplied infinitely
and he attributes to himself blame for commissions and omissions. His conviction of failure is often delusionary and filled
with terror and blackness. His own exaggerations overwhelm
him, and in his depressed behavior he outwardly seeks to exon-
erate himself and to protect himself by frequently whimpering
and crying.

Manic States

   The manic phase of this same malady is more obvious in its
defensive approach. The manic employs a whole range of protective behavior. His exterior behavior is hyperactive, full of excitement and agitation. His interior confusion and anguish is no
less intense or different than in the depressed state, but is simply
manifested in an opposite manner. The manic does not plead,
but attacks his imaginary assailants through every possible chan-
nel. He talks incessantly in a high-pitched voice. He raves and
rants on topics related to his conflict either directly or indirectly.
He moves constantly, performs useless activities for hours at a
time, and frequently his whole being seems to be convulsed by
the movements of his body. He seems to derive his best satisfactions from sheer activity, vehemently resisting ordinary amounts
of sleep or rest. His speech is extremely irascible, his mannerisms are hasty, and his walk is rapid. His movements are shaky
and uncoordinated, reflecting his inner confusion. He ventilates
his accumulated defenses haphazardly in all directions.
   The manic also exteriorizes himself in dramatic pretentious
roles. To defend the impoverished ego which he cannot endure,
he becomes a great figure who commands respect and esteem.
He foists himself upon others by identifying himself in name
and gesture with some heroic, noble, or praiseworthy person-
age. In this way he commands others and directs and controls
his fantasy world. Not having sufficient identity within his own
self, he embraces another ego. Through the make-believe ego,
he channels his hyperactivity by expressions that reveal many aspects of his struggle for self-assertion. Unable to reinforce his
own subjective strength, he moves out of himself and into another by delusionary means.
   The manic-depressive represents an extreme disorientation

arising from conflicts in personal relationships, different in origin from those of the schizophrenic. The movement of the manic-depressive is outward instead of inward. He discharges his dynamic energies without direction or purpose. He literally spends himself, and in his frenzied dissipations he is so self-involved that he is unable to receive or to reciprocate. In the early beginnings he was more interested in expressing himself than in permitting others to express themselves, more eager to talk than to listen, more engrossed in self than in another. Accumulated mechanisms of this type gradually lead to impairment of human relationships; the manic-depressive becomes unable to relate to or *for* another, and he resorts to his mental defenses. He *extends* himself; but does not move toward *becoming*.

Paranoid States

The occurrence of pure paranoia, which has sometimes been designated as the third type of major psychogenic disorders, is practically nonexistent in current case studies. In recent research paranoid tendencies are usually combined with schizophrenic disorders or psychopathology. However, in the paranoid patient, the dynamic movement includes other qualitative aspects than those we have observed in schizophrenia and in manic-depression. While the schizophrene withdraws, regresses, and inverts his energies toward himself, the paranoid draws to himself instead of withdrawing. There is an important qualitative difference in these two dynamic functions, even though they exist in parallel fashion within the same patient. The dominantly paranoid person might be described as unable to give, but voracious in receiving. His energies are directed into many areas to receive, and always in inordinate ways. What he receives he wants to possess entirely to the point of consumption. He does not receive another for the sake of the other but entirely for himself. Jealousy and ambition become seething torrents within him and are the chief impediments to self-awareness. The paranoid is unusually keen and perceptive in regard to whatever satiates his inward burning. His alertness to objective reality, insofar as it pertains to his ends, is remarkably clear and sensitive.

His orientation to the world outside of himself is apparently realistic, but actually is distorted by the delusions that form strong networks in his thinking. The paranoid's delusions are more internalized than those of other mentally disturbed patients, and are built upon persons or situations perceived as interferences in his demented designs. Delusions of persecution and destruction are the most common dynamisms dominating the paranoid. The compelling desire in the paranoid to possess everything for himself is the most distinctive one, and impairs his human relationships; it is also capable of endangering others. The paranoid derives exhilarating satisfaction in the experience of destructive behavior. His internal world of fantasy also does not suffice, but stimulates his aberrations. The world of things as it exists outside of himself does not fulfill him because he cannot relate to it, but must take it to himself. When the paranoid can accumulate, absorb, and be engrossed in what he takes or receives, his urgencies are relieved, but only temporarily. Paranoid satisfactions often arouse more diffused needs and aggravate his problem.

The psychic movement of energies within the paranoid are as lopsided and imbalanced as they are in other disorders. His deviant behavior is also an attempt to build an impoverished ego and is directed to drawing objects to himself; he exercises an exaggerated, extreme type of receiving. Distorted emotional habits have resulted in an ego functioning seriously warped rather than merely deficient.

NEUROSES

We have described the flow of energy in the major psychogenic disorders as directional movement of the total personality outward, inward, or consuming. The neuroses are best understood in view of a dominant directional energy within their mode of relating. The problems in communication and interpersonal relationships in the neuroses are severe, but not to the same degree as in the psychoses. The personality is impaired, but not with such global results. Neurotics suffer difficulties in relationships but, in general, they still continue to maintain some personal ties with others. Their disfunctioning does not remove them so completely from the social environment of family and associates.

The total personality retains a certain coordination of its entirety but is unable to function effectively because of prolonged emotional disturbances. Neurotic actions are related to the dominance of one or two negative emotions more than to an entire system of disintegrating habits, and to a weak self rather than to a distorted self.

The neurotic personalities exhibit their problems in relatedness through different channels and in symptomatic behavior predominantly physical in some cases, predominantly psychic in others. Regardless of the differing symptoms, all neuroses arise from deep-seated anxiety. In modern research we speak of the anxiety states because anxiety is at the root of all neuroses. The personality in its movement toward becoming is paralyzed by a pervading anxiety which circulates through its psychological arteries. In his attempts to be, to become, and to relate to others, the neurotic is gripped with a growing apprehension, often more distressing because it is indefinable. The insecure self must first weigh and balance each movement in terms of its risk. The whole vista of otherness is minutely calculated in terms of threats to the self. The flow of self is restricted before it begins. The neurotic differs precisely at this point from the psychotic. He has greater awareness of others, of his own situation, and of the surrounding universe. He wants to relate to others, but his volitions and desires are stifled by the trepidation that dominates his subjective movements. These habits are basically self-centered and interfere with both giving and receiving.

The neurotic personality relates to others in a very limited and constricted way. The joy of sharing is overshadowed by a prevailing fear. The approach to others is clouded by hesitation and doubts. Often, overwhelming guilt feelings cause the neurotic to be so rejecting and hostile that he inflicts pain on others with whom he associates. Enveloped in fear, and often in anger and despair, the neurotic personality operates negatively toward others. Neurotic movements are predominantly shunning, avoiding, regretting, declining, refusing. Many movements in the neurotic personality are strong and active, but concentrate on methods of unwholesome restraint. Energies are uselessly inhibited instead of productively directed. The problem of the neurotic personality is the restriction of dynamic movement. But the ways of developing habits of retaining energies, instead of directing them, vary greatly. Some are habituated to specific subjective habits such as we see in the obsessive-compulsive neurotics; others resort to physical patterns including generalized physical inabilities such as aches, pains, and debilitating maladies. The hysterical conversions, previously common, have practically disappeared in our times. All neurotic personalities are afflicted with generalized and pervading anxieties.

Obsessive-Compulsive States

In the obsessive-compulsive neurotic, the power of dynamic energy is unmistakable. The patient is usually aware of the nonsensical nature of his compulsive movements. He sees the ill effects they have on his relationships with others but is unable to direct this pent-up energy as he wishes. His anguish is acute as he realizes the ridiculous activities in which he indulges, always against his own desires. The drive to perform this or that repetitive action is greater than he is. He feels engulfed by an urgency that surges up within him, and forces him to retrace his steps, to reread the page, to reexamine his room countless times. His hands and feet seem to perform all of these routine actions while he remains a helpless observer. He feels outside of himself, and his body performs without him, automatically, monotonously, uselessly. The dichotomy is not complete, because once the procedure has been finished, he can grasp the reins a little and steer again, but not for long. This is the loneliness of the compulsive; forced into a rut of mechanical performances he personally rejects, separated from satisfactory communication with others by restrictions he cannot escape, and suffering from what he often sees but cannot remedy. He knows that he does not relate well with others and he wants to do so, but is impeded by his own inner constrictions.

The obsessive counterpart experiences much the same impulse, except that his constrictive habits are confined more to his ideational functions. It is hardly possible to separate these two neurotic forms, since they imply a reciprocal movement within and without the person. In describing his experiences, the obsessive person refers to the persistence of an idea. The obsessed neurotic is haunted by the phantoms of ideas that churn within him day after day. Whatever he does or wherever he goes, the same imagery or the same idea remains in front of him, often with eidetic clarity. It pursues him relentlessly, and sometimes his only relief comes from behavioral expression in some bizarre form. Absorbed by inner thoughts, the neurotic is completely tied up within. His preoccupation with self leaves little room for thought of others, and his relationships are fragmentary, since he is incapable of sustained ideas that pertain to others. His conversations and actions are invaded by the ideas that hold sway within. In all of his relationships with others, as well as in his own self-fulfillment as a person, he is hindered by thinking he cannot control or direct.

In compulsive activities the neurotic feels estranged from his actions. They continue in spite of himself. In obsessive activities the intensity of estrangement is even greater. The obsessive experiences an inner aloneness often excruciating, because his obsessed ideas are so intimately himself and yet not himself. One of the most common forms of compulsive behavior is scrupulosity. Guilt feelings, in reality unrelated to sin or moral guilt, spring from the neurotic's perseverant need to relieve himself, to cleanse himself symbolically of something he wants to get rid of. His weakened ego and insufficient sense of identity are unable to support the responsibilities that would provide the security he needs. He hesitates, and doubts, but does not decide. He shelters himself under another's certitude. Faced with decisions, he experiences panic and indulges in peculiar deviations to avoid the issue. He quickly seeks refuge by shifting the responsibility to another and in order to achieve this end he may use many odd tactics. The scrupulous person is inordinately concerned with details because he busies himself with trifles to avoid the threat of broader issues. He is unlikely to distinguish well between important principles and nonessentials. He does not perceive irrelevant and insignificant items as such because his intellectual vision is clouded. He does not see things in perspective but rather looks at them through a magnifying glass. In his human relationships, his own self-absorption takes priority and he finds it difficult to meet the personal needs of others or to judge situations from their viewpoint. The scrupulous person is compelled by inner urgencies to seek relief in ritualistic performances, which fill his life; his outlook is geared to object-relations rather than to subject-relations.

Some neurotic personalities may experience fewer of these compelling energies and more of a diffused anxiety, less tangible, but always there. Obsessive ideas may be absent, but thinking in general is permeated with fear. The confirmed pessimist who sees everything in a negative light, the skeptical and mistrusting person, are examples of neurotics whose mentality is steeped in fearful habits, but not chained by compulsive behavior.

General Anxiety States

Diffused anxiety is not as acute as in the obsessive-compulsive type, but is just as distressing, and can break the continuity of good human relationships. The fearful outlook sees the ominous and foreboding lurking on the horizon. When some joyful event occurs, the neurotic sees in this happiness something ominous. Appreciating good things in life and participating in joy is almost impossible, since whatever favorable events occur are viewed as portents of misfortune. It is better not to enjoy or hope, and thus avoid the inevitable suffering that must follow. For the neurotic, joy means suffering, hope means disappointment. All emotions take a negative direction. The dynamic system is heavily overloaded with movements that play safe but do not sustain. In his constant efforts to save his endangered ego, the neurotic severs the very source of his own growth. His affiliations are superficial and short-lived because he cannot freely join with others. He gives of himself in a miserly way, and measures all that he receives. Often, like a child, he gives in order to receive, and misses the value in the act of giving itself. The dynamic joy of giving to another holds no attraction for the fear-ridden neurotic. Since he is unstable in his own resources, giving to others is painful and only increases his feeling of loss. He is more able to dispense of things than to give of himself, but in either case the process is difficult for him.

The pervasive anxiety of the neurotic causes him to be overwhelmed by loneliness. His future is filled with impending darkness and the present is confined to his dull existence. He feels alone and deprived. He is torn between the risks that the company of others involves, and the intolerable confinement of his own rigidity. The loneliness he endures in these struggles sometimes gives him sensations of an interior "crumbling," as if he cannot withstand the pressures of either alternative. The neurotic feels isloated in his narrow confines and cut off from others by his incapacity to share and cooperate. Nor can he find a way to be recognized or esteemed, since he can do little else than perform his routine rituals. He is afraid of himself, his fears, and all that surround him. The terror that the severely neurotic patient suffers from the strangulating effects of his own fears reduces him to helplessness. He cannot open himself to others, and the anguish of his aloneness almost paralyzes his already restricted activities. The neurotic is caught in his own vicious circle of anxiety, fostering more anxiety patterns, and his hope of recovery lies in therapy.

In addition, the neurotic has vivid sensations of emptiness and he constructs intricate behavior patterns understood in the light of this fundamental theme. His exaggerated need for things, quantities, his habits of storing, or hoarding, or miserliness, useless saving and scrutinizing economy may rotate around an intense feeling of hollowness within and a void without. Anxiety tends to drain him of everything. The stress of anxiety in the self-reflection of magnified deficiencies, of omissions, of gaps, of vacancies, brings an overwhelming sense of emptiness. The deprivations realized through weak or broken human relationships leave him emotionally impoverished.

Neurotic problems also reflect the deeper struggles of the culture in which we live. The depersonalizing systems of many large industries, and the mechanization of living in our century are some of the major sources of neurotic habits. The emptiness felt by the neurotic goes hand in hand with the boredom of his meager existence. He is not sufficient for himself and has not developed enough inner security to satisfy his own needs. By curtailing meaningful relations with others, he is left with the monotonous routine he has constructed. His life becomes stagnant, and the awareness of its futility, and severe inflexibility without any defined purpose, leaves him emotionally deprived. The neurotic's awareness of his ineffectual living and his apparent inability to cope with it or improve it brings on a deadening sense of futility. The dynamic system craves an outlet, and cooped up within a regime that is stultifying instead of challenging, the neurotic finds relief through many devices.

The pervading anxiety of all the neurotic states undermines the personality strength in such a way as to make it inflexible. Personality increases by multiple extensions and *becomes* by forward movements. The neurotic remains static because of his anxiety. To grow and increase, the personality must meet new openings for expression, different channels for the flow of its dynamic energy. Anxiety serves to block these outflowings of self and to invert the movement back upon the self. In the flood of loneliness, emptiness, dissipated energy caused by anxiety, the self becomes damaged and incompetent.

Even though movements toward growth in the neurotic personality are arrested or retarded, the movements of the inner self continue and pass through other outlets. Anxiety in itself is a powerful dynamic energy and functions strongly within the neurotic personality. Its negative course forces the neurotic to exhibit himself in many types of unwholesome ways. Pervasive anxiety also manifests itself through physical and bodily infirmities. When anxiety is released through these modes, the ailments are numerous, continual, and find little relief in medicinal remedies. The physical problems are functional rather than organic in origin, and while the neurotic depends on many medical remedies, his maladies do not subside. The physical indispositions of neurotics are generalized in aches and pains of all kinds, in exhaustion and fatigue. His suffering from these afflictions is real; but the afflictions come from functional reflections of his anxiety, and not from specific organic disorders.

Any experience of anxiety is fatiguing, as everyone understands well. The endurance of grief, worry, and anxious situations are more depleting than strenuous physical exertions. The neurotic experiences no relief from anxiety because it is so diffused. It pervades his whole inner self and becomes interwoven into everything he thinks, feels, and does. He continually complains of overfatigue and gives this as the cause of his inability to associate with others in ordinary affairs, or to maintain a job. He is unreliable in his duties and performs them with a lack of interest and with mediocre results. His whole approach to work, action, and to meeting others lacks enthusiasm and vitality. In reality his physical health may be excellent, but his anxiety prevents him from enjoying it and using it for achievement of positive goals. His physical qualities as well as his mental capabilities are enmeshed in the grip of anxiety that makes him restless, agitated, and unstable. The movement of the inner self is expended uselessly within itself. It is wasted by constrictions that intensify confusion, and by complexes revolving in a limited orbit. Energies find outlets only in distressing compulsions, obsessions, acute loneliness, or physical problems.

These are brief descriptions of the neurotic patterns in their subjectivity. These are the experiential processes that render neurotics ineffectual in personality expressions in communicating and in interpersonal relationships.

PSYCHOGENIC ORIGINS

The dynamisms that begin early in life or in the incipient stages of psychoses and neuroses are the real sources of these major breaks in human relationships. Growing in strength through habitual exercise, they often converge as the person uses more and more of them in his techniques of escape, defense, or self-acquisition. Mental dynamisms take on momentum and serve to damage the self instead of expanding it. In the interest of prevention it is important for the person himself to become aware early of what is going on within. His behavior patterns are only exterior ways of communicating himself, and what is more important to him and to others is "what he is trying to communicate." When the forms of communication are inadequate and the person is unsuccessful in most of his relationships, his difficulties lie within. It is comparatively easy for a person to become aware of these dynamisms in their first beginnings, but it becomes a difficult and unraveling process as they grow in complexity. We will gain insight into harmful mental dynamisms and early forms of inadequate interchange if we are sensitive to these experiential meanings.

Perhaps our failure to prevent the progression of unwholesome dynamisms in their incipient stages is due to our lack of sensitivity to their subjective origins. What we see as an external manifestation of obstinancy, resentment, piety, social interest, may have more significant dimensions in their interior meanings. The response may be accurate as it stands objectively, but the understanding of the experiential dimension will enhance the value of this response, will render the same answer more meaningful, more indicative of a wider reality. When we look at a postcard of a beautiful landscape we miss the perspective; looking at the same picture with visual depth gives us a better appreciation of its beauty. The three-dimensional view may not be as beautiful as the reality perceived directly, but it certainly gives us a better view of the landscape as it really exists. Similarly, in personality, objective responses and exterior media give us one dimension of this dynamic capacity, a flat-surface view. This one dimension may be adequate. But as it is realized along with the other multidimensional depths of subjective experience it will undoubtedly be seen in a different perspective.

This openness to another's subjectivity will enable us to communicate more freely with him and to exchange more readily. This is what is meant by trying to understand another by entering into his world. To receive and accept another we must first try to see things from his mind's eye, from his frame of reference. In many cases we will not be able to agree or to adopt these interpretations. Agreement or adoption is not necessary for exchange, but openness and acceptance are essential. It is possible to enter the world of another without remaining there; it is possible to appreciate another's interpretation without incorporating it. For the other it is important that we understand, not necessarily that we imitate what we come to know.

To understand a child, one must forget for a time all the adult approaches, and endeavor to see the world through the child's vision. His highly imaginative mental life embraces many fantasies that have receded from the adult's consciousness. But it is through this perceptual realm that he evaluates and expresses himself. To interpret his behavior, and to know him, we must know his inner thinking and feeling. With the young child it is more difficult because his verbalization is limited. But our openness to him, our wanting to understand him, enlarges our receptivity and, in turn, increases his expressiveness. We must learn what certain objects mean to him. Trinkets useless for the adult, broken or discarded articles, may be treasures for the child. In his imagination he may have built great castles on these useless items. An adult, heedless of the child's feelings, may shatter a collection of objects worthless in themselves but invaluable in the child's world.

The teenager's world is neither that of the child nor of the adult. To know him we must be able to live in his orbit and to meet him there. We cannot expect the adolescent to meet us on an adult basis because he has not yet arrived there. But maturity is more flexible and yielding, and should be able to communicate with him on his own level. The adult sees values and goals geared toward the future; but the teenager finds it difficult to grasp these firmly because he is so vitally of the present. We lead him to an appreciation for the future only through proximate steps that lie in his time zone. We cannot reach the child through adult appeals, but we can reach him if we are open to his interests, to his desires and dreams. When we crush his unrealistic aspirations we have lost our contact with him, but when we have been free and open to his exaggerations, and to his extravagant plans, we have communicated with him. For the teenager, the realization of his absurd proposals is not what is important; it is the receptivity that is extended to him that is so vital. He exercises his natural skepticism by testing and trying the adults who guide him, and what he really wants to know is their degree of tolerance, the depth of their understanding, not their willingness to fulfill absurd projects.

With children and adolescents whose personalities have not yet matured, and for neurotics and psychotics whose personalities have become disintegrated, openness and receptivity will be one-sided. They need support but cannot give of themselves in return. They are dependent on others for fulfillment and growth. With them the challenge of openness and extension is greater and more difficult since it requires a more profound grasp of subjectivity and a wider range of sensitivity to others. Counseling and psychotherapy are the only channels through which personality growth and change can be accomplished.

Ch

THE ROLE OF THE COUNSELOR

The client's most crucial need is his first contact with the counselor; it is the beginning of hope. The significance of the first meetng cannot be overestimated, since the client's experience of relief at this moment will indicate its meaningfulness to him. Alleviation of pain in the presence of the counselor will make an aperture in the barriers which separate the client from others. He will see a glimpse of assurance in the world of otherness, and perhaps realize in a small way that renewal of life and freedom is restored by relating to others rather than being absorbed in self. The desire for sustained otherness, for continued renewal, will depend on the awakening the counselor inspires. The first interview, especially, requires the courage and cooperation of the client. Of himself he has little; but from the acceptance of the counselor he receives assurance. Lacking fundamental security, his first contact with the counselor is filled with portent and he experiences dread and misgiving. Perhaps it will mean greater pain, more confusion. Depressing thoughts fill his consciousness. The counselor, then, in the first session, must impart a certain feeling of confidence and communicate warmth with an invitation to relinquish estrangement from others.

ATTITUDES OF THE COUNSELOR

The attitudes of the counselor, more than any other means, will convey the responsiveness the client seeks. His ability to inspire confidence in the client depends more on his own subjectivity, his readiness to receive, than on outlined techniques. It is important that the counselor have a keen insight into his own inner feelings in order to marshal their assistance. The counselor will not always be free of anxiety, hostility or other negative feelings in regard to himself or his situation; but his awareness of them will enable him to utilize them or at least to prevent them from interfering with therapy.

Having reached the status of counselor through intensive training and mastering of fundamental psychological principles, the therapist is also dependent on his inner sources for success. There is a certain limit even the best training reaches in preparing the counselor for his tasks. Beyond this point the skill of the counselor depends on his reservoir, his own effectiveness as a person. There is a certain indefinable quality that distinguishes an excellent therapist from an ordinary or mediocre counselor. We use the term "personableness" to describe this gift or simply refer to the counselor's ability to communicate. A thorough education and high caliber training does not necessarily guarantee this personal asset, even though most training programs eliminate candidates who are not suitable. Psychiatrists and clinical psychologists by virtue of their titles have completed the requirements for this status. But there are still many psychiatrists and psychologists who are not superior therapists. Some are more talented in research than in therapy.

The counselor, then, in his capacity as therapist, requires a certain inexplicable disposition, arising from his own uniqueness and refined by his training which enables him to be *for* the client, to fill him with confidence and hope. The therapist needs a certain innate sensitivity to the unverbalized needs and a keen intuition of the subjectivity of others. This inherent awareness, together with his disciplined proficiency, enables him to approach the distressed person with insight and competence. The counselor faces the delicate task of perceiving anguish in its multidimensional aspects. He must recognize the rhythm and flux, unique in this personality, but yet related to the general movement of all human energy.

The counselor, in his approach to the client, must be cognizant of the intricacies of human sensibilities and of the delicacy of his task as he ventures into the realm of another. He cannot suddenly destroy props and reverse the direction of energy. Much less can he attempt to break down the facade or bulwarks the client has constructed. The client cannot be thrust out of his refuge. The counselor's task is to be a person, a source of relatedness, and for this engagement he must have sufficient self-knowledge of his own. All that his educational and scientific training has given him he himself must have assimilated dynamically. He must have a certain *feeling* for what he knows, a certain existential awareness of the skills he has acquired. His savoir-faire depends on an inner compass that guides him into unknown territory and gauges the fragility of the client's tolerance. There are no standard instruments he can select from without to help him explore the subjectivity of another, because his task is not to explore an object but to meet another person.

The attitudes of the counselor will be his strongest assets or greatest pitfalls. Approaching a client with an investigating attitude, a questioning frame of mind will effect a certain withdrawal and enkindle more fearfulness. Probing pushes the patient against the wall and tends to engender more hostility. The client needs and seeks another person, and the counselor in his own consciousness must be filled with awareness of being this person. The favorable attitudes that best equip the counselor include everything that "being a person" means for the client. His regard for the client must contain all the dispositions of outwardness to another person; acceptance, respect, esteem, reverence.

The attitudes of the counselor will depend much on his own concepts of a human person. Unconscious experiences as well as our conscious activities strongly influence our relationships with others. The counselor's attitudes toward his client will be governed by basic concepts in his theory of counseling, notions of personality, philosophy of life. Convictions based on mechanistic interpretations of man will bias the attitudes of the counselor, for mechanism is concerned more with an operator and ability to manipulate skillfully. An attitude of manipulation will not perceive the client as subject, but rather in the capacity of an object to be remolded. An attitude of this kind will not enhance the ensuing relationship and the client will inevitably feel himself being *moved* instead of *received*. The counselor who hopes to see the client progress toward self-direction will only retard the process by "moving" him as an object. It is the self-movement of the counselee that eventually achieves success. The counselor's concern for the development and self-functioning in the client is essential in providing an atmosphere of freedom and is an invitation to use it without fear.

The responses these different attitudes will evoke are significant as the client tries to feel his ground and grasps blindly in the confusion of his emotions. He will pick up the counselor's dispositions quickly and be deeply affected by them. He will react as "object" if he senses an operational approach in his counselor. Instinctively he will follow this role instead of experiencing a sense of alleviation. Unable consciously to distinguish between the role of object and the experience of being subject in its true sense, he will instinctively follow the lead that is given.

Left to his own resources, even in his confusion, the client will react in the capacity of subject if he experiences diminished anguish. The acuteness of his feelings makes him more receptive to an attitude that imparts acknowledgment of his person, because his pain has been caused by forlornness and estrangement. Others have forsaken him and forgotten that he is a person. Suffering has come to him from the loss of contact with himself as a person. Security in regard to his own being has been shattered and he wonders what he really is. The firm recognition of his person received from another assuages his discomfort; he feels for the first time that he is significant, that he conveys meaning to another in his capacity as a person. Through the accepting regard of the counselor, the client senses the solace of another's interest and esteem. An awareness of being someone, of being this someone whom another recognizes as important, worthy of notice and attention, eases his pain. To accomplish these first stirrings of hope, the counselor himself must possess strong attitudes of appreciation for the client as a unique being capable of self-direction.

Counselor Self-Awareness

The counselor's openness to the client must include a willingness to understand him, to listen attentively to what he says, and to be interested in what this means to the counselee. He must thoroughly understand what the client says in order to respond. In order to transmit his desire to be of help, he must be genuinely and favorably disposed toward the client, for whatever basic sentiments he has for this person in particular are revealed in his approach and are quickly perceived.

Emotionally upset people are unusually keen and perceptive, and quickly absorb the general mood of the counseling situation. The client, in self-protection, searches and scrutinizes the counselor for flaws and defects. Like everything else, the counselor is a thing or object in his world, and he observes to see how he operates. He enters the situation full of doubts and fears, prone to negative thinking, skeptical of the outcome, and expects reproach and rejection. When he discovers a person who responds to his mistrust with assurance and confidence instead of the expected disapproval and hostility, he is disarmed and relaxes some of his defenses. The positive demeanor of the counselor, implying receptivity, leaves the client with stirrings of hope and joy, and the satisfaction from these first glimpses of certainty induces the client to accept the invitation to communicate with another.

Counselor Self-Acceptance

The counselor must be aware of his own inner feelings and accept them. If he himself is at odds within, struggling with interior problems, he will find it difficult to be accepting and interested in the client. However, when he finds that he is unavoidably filled with strong feelings and tends to be distracted by them, his own acceptance of these feelings, his own willingness to recognize the sentiments that prevail, will help him to be genuine in his relations to the client. Before he can be accepting of another he must first be accepting of himself. Each counselor will discover certain methods that will facilitate self-awareness and self-acceptance. Realizing that self-acceptance is important in the presence of negative feelings helps to prevent accumulation of tensions. The counselor will have blind spots and prejudices; he may also have habitual tensions and complexes. These problems will not seriously interfere with his efficiency if he can recognize and accept them. There is no perfect man, no perfect counselor. On the contrary, the counselor aware of his own shortcomings is more able to grasp the suffering of the client. Only when the counselor is unwilling to be realistic within himself and is not aware of his deficiencies is he limited by them.

Aware of and accepting his own inner conflicts and tensions, he will be open to the client's reaction to him and will not be fearful when the client reacts negatively. In being ready for the client's hostile responses, he will not be defensive or retaliating.

The counselor's recognition of his own personal enrichment in knowing and communicating with another influences his disposition toward the client. This acknowledgment will enhance his interest and widen his perspective. Realizing the values, not merely pragmatically but also for their own worth, the counselor will experience an increase of freedom himself. It is the feeling of freedom that gives the counselor a sense of affinity for the subjectivity of another. In his freedom his attitudes are fluent without being vacillating; he maintains his equilibrium but is able to move along with the client in his shifts of moods, in his fragmented and complex verbalizations. Free from self-distraction, his focus is clear and penetrating and his capacity for acceptance of another enlarged.

The more the counselor strives for freedom and utilizes it, the more truly is he himself. In being himself he imparts genuineness to the client, who is strengthened by the reality that the true self represents. When a person is not really himself he doesn't ring true and the emotionally upset person recognizes this lack of authenticity. A weak personal autonomy in a counselor is obvious to the client because he is searching for stability as a guidepost for himself. The signs of personality defenses and protective devices are the cues the client knows best, because he has become familiar with them. He may not have good self-insight, but he quickly perceives the shields and camouflages in others. The counselor does not succeed well in helping another toward finding himself if he does not establish real relationships with the client. His self-direction must be steady but not superficial; he must be aware of his true feelings and not try to convey the opposite.

For example, the counselor cannot afford to mask his feelings, to pretend to be impervious to fatigue, impenetrable to adverse conditions. His acceptance of these limitations and also his acceptance of the client's perception of them will help him to avoid superficial relatedness. Two requisites go hand in hand to prepare for good rapport: complete acceptance of self and complete acceptance of the client and his inner world.

Once the counselor has mastered his attitudes of acceptance, he can move freely along in the flow of events. The meeting between counselor and counselee is the beginning of a process that changes and evolves constantly, and the agility of the counselor in adapting to these changes is essential to the client's welfare. Rigid attitudes become stationary blocks and hinder progress. Any form of nonacceptance becomes a barrier and creates a tendency in the counselor to direct the client as an object. Nonaccepting attitudes in the counselor lessen the client's self-confidence. When a counselor feels insecure he takes the reins and wants to change the course. If he begins to direct and manipulate, he can interrupt the advance and injure the client's renewal of hope. It is not the occurrence of limitations that are so harmful, but the inability to accept them that wreaks havoc. For a denial of reality in any slight way causes a cessation of progress, and it is only through the movement of change that the client arrives at newness of spirit.

COUNSELOR SELF-DIRECTION

Many other individual attitudes exist that may lessen the counselor's security, and each person by himself will know these weaknesses best. One other general source of insecurity is an attitude of feeling responsible for the client's self-direction. This attitude can develop anxiety and the counselor will tend to be hasty and seek the most available solutions. In doing so he tries more to alleviate his own anxiety than to provide an opportunity for change. The counselor can offer a situation to the client, but he cannot change things for him. The client's personal cooperation and entrance into involvement within the counseling situation is his own contribution and cannot be forced.

In assuming responsibility for another, the counselor again takes things into his own hands, tries to fix things up, to put them in order. When he is anxious about the client's progress he tends to shape the relationship, which is easier to do than to be patient in awaiting and attending. The client himself, within his deepest subjectivity, is capable of knowing best the nature of his conflicts. He may often know the best means of reaching a solution. It is not the potential for awareness that is lacking, but the actualization that is unachieved. The solution lies within his reach but out of his sight. The counselor's responsibility is not to take action for the client, but, by his presence, to provide the occasion, the opportunity for the client to move toward self-direction.

The counselor's responsibility toward himself, and his acceptance of that responsibility, is an attitude of being *present*, ready to respond to the client's forward movement. It is the freedom to be responsible that the client seeks, slowly but surely. The feeling of another's strength brings courage and reassurance as he falters and wavers in his struggle with conflicting motives. But the manipulations of the counselor could remove this chance and the client may be confused by mixed feelings of relief and loss. His final achievement of strong identity and self-direction will not come from release of self-responsibility, but from the exhilarating satisfaction of freely choosing his own plan and executing it with confidence.

One's most satisfying human relationships evolve from interchange with real people. The more authentic a person is, the more stable the bonds he forms with others. In much the same way, the client needs the counselor as an authentic person. He does not require nor seek some *thing* from the counselor, even though his own ideas about counseling may be vague and uncertain. But in the depths of his being, his whole self evinces his needs and deficiencies. His insecurity seeks solidity; his doubts search for certitude; his agitation looks for tranquility and his fluctuating ego wants identity. The satisfaction for these initial needs can be attained only by the felt-knowledge of these attributes as they exist in another person. The client arrives at self-awareness and self-direction only through an existential experience with another authentic person.

In general, then, the attitudes of the counselor include the dispositions which will enable him to lead the client from his state of suffering and confusion to one of movement toward effective living. With his own positive feelings of acceptance and interest, the counselor hopes to assuage the client's suffering in his subjection to negative emotions. Whatever professional positive experience the counselor can provide for the client helps him to taste the delights of joy, hope, and love. Denied these over a long period of time, he has become ensnared in a dense maze of negative feelings; he is overwhelmed. Realizing the positive attitudes of the counselor, he comes to see how they function, to know them in operation, to know them as they really exist. The client gradually senses that the presence of the counselor evokes a change within him. The solace he yearns for comes within more and more proximate range. As the horizon clarifies, he envisions the final goal and the distance he must cover to reach it. Slowly but steadily, through the felt-knowledge of the equilibrium that has formed within him, he moves forward, and the negative dominance of anguish, confusion, incredulity recedes and the self emerges renewed and regained.

THE COUNSELING RELATIONSHIP

It is difficult to describe the different aspects of a counseling situation, part by part, because in reality it is a process that includes many movements functioning simultaneously. However, now we can attempt to concentrate on the exchange that occurs. In every counseling session there is the client with all of his subjctive suffering, the therapist with his receptive attitudes, and the interpersonal exchange which becomes the heart of the matter, the primary purpose of counseling.

Counseling is the process wherein the counselor enters into a relationship with the client for the purpose of offering the opportunity of existential experience in personal growth. The counselor in relating to the client does not give him help but strives *to be of help*. The differentiation here is important. The counselor, by his being a real person, by his attitudes of acceptance toward the client, and by his understanding, offers himself to the client as another human individual who wants to be *for* him, to be of help, to be the other to whom the client can relate with confidence. The counseling process begins with the first meeting when the counselor, by his warmth, produces a psychological climate that relieves some of the acute pain that bewilders the client.

As has been noted, the importance of the client's first contact with the counselor cannot be overemphasized. In this first approach he must realize the possibility of relief and hope in his relationship with the counselor. For success there must be mutual exchange; the client must cooperate in order to improve. Even though he is rigidly constricted by his own struggles he possesses a certain potential for cooperation. If he does not reciprocate and respond to the invitation that the counselor extends, the counseling process will not occur. The counselor does not give a *thing* to the client, he does not impose words, or present advice; he relates to the client. If he does this successfully, the client responds, very minimally in the beginning, but gradually more and more as the process continues.

The therapist relates to the client and extends himself as a genuine person; the ways of doing so differ according to his own philosophy and theory. The phenomenological emphasis does not exclude a variety of approaches but merely suggests focus that accentuates the meaningfulness of becoming an effective person. The orientations to therapy are numerous, e.g., psychoanalysis, Rogerian, self-actualization theory, Adlerian and Jungian approaches, the logotherapeutic system, and many others. The counselor's concept of person and his basic psychological convictions will guide his preferred methods of approach. Over and above these is the emphasis stressing the client's primary need to become a person, to realize identity, and to experience an existential relationship with another human being. No matter what the orientation may be, the counseling process must provide this true relationship which enables the client to reach for maturity and to develop an effective personality. If he does not achieve this, the counseling process has not been completely successful.

An approach that begins with diagnostic techniques, as some do, interpretative or investigating measures, will run the risk of failure from the beginning. The client is threatened by other *things*, by attempts to manipulate him as an object. His whole range of experiences has been a sequence of self-deprivation. His confusion and misery are results of his inner rebellion against being reduced to an object. He wants to become free, to know another, to realize the joy of interchange in the dignity of his person. A diagnostic or investigative technique may be just one more unpleasant episode to increase his pain instead of lessening it. The counselor's offer of warmth and receptivity is far more meaningful to him than a set of diagnostics that may enhance the counselor's knowledge but leaves the client feeling cold, used, and more dismembered than before. For the client the human contact is the most significant; it is from the counselor, as this interested person, that he receives comfort and a certain sense of regained newness. Counseling, then, is essentially an interpersonal exchange and must begin with the first moment of greeting, must continue with each session and conclude with the client's growth from a self-deprived object to a self-integrated subject.

The therapist himself must distinguish carefully between his techniques and his own understanding of this specific person. He derives these from his personal contacts in counseling. His own knowledge of skills and interpretations of systems and types will tend to be constructive, and may be used for assimilation and evaluation after the counseling session has terminated. But in the actual session, during the exchange between himself and the client, the counselor must use his knowledge to participate, to encourage the client to share himself as he reveals his feelings. Shared experiences and the feeling of participation will be less threatening to the client. However, he will know and understand new dimensions of being in terms of reality only by participation. It helps him to know that he is not being victimized and that no matter how grotesque his fantasies, no matter how bizarre his ideas, or violent his feelings, he is not just pouring all of this out for someone to know and analyze. The tensions becomes less acute when he can expose his deepest sentiments with confidence and know that all are being warmly received and accepted rather than analyzed and interpreted. He prefers the empathy of the counselor to his analysis. He is not interested in how much knowledge the counselor has about him or how skillfully he interprets what he says; it is the felt response of the counselor that is more significant.

NEEDS OF THE CLIENT

The client seeks to know freedom, to learn how to choose, to exercise his responsibilities. The defenses he has built up over a long period of time are substitutes for reality and bring no satisfaction. His dynamisms of escape have reduced him as a person, making him feel worthless, guilty, and incapable. Confined within his own limited structures, he looks to the counselor for a way out. To regain his freedom, he must know what freedom is, and how to attain it. First of all, he must experience it in order to make it his own. The counselor, then, establishes this atmosphere of freedom and openness, not by words, but through his attitudes and the receptivity he expresses; by his whole being, his inner and outer self, he lets the client *feel* freedom, lets him be himself, lets him say what he wants, feel what he wants. In his face and by his whole manner he shows the client that he understands and feels for him. In so doing he gives the client the chance freely to express himself without being condemned, blamed, or despised. The client, in being himself, freely revealing himself, and at the same time feeling the response of acceptance and understanding, realizes in his inner being a sense of freedom, the real freedom of his own person, and being accepted as such without need of artificial superstructures.

Little by little, as the client continues to disclose his feelings, realizing that he can be accepted by another human being in his individual dignity without facades, he begins to relinquish them. Through his participation of the experience of freedom he is enlightened, and knows that the false fronts that he has erected are useless, that they are not necessary for his welfare, that they diminish his freedom instead of enlarging it. He soon discards them when they no longer serve a purpose. They were developed to guard his insecurity; hence when he feels assurance within himself he no longer depends on unrealistic stratagems. He adopts the modes and means of freedom learned through therapy. He experiences these as satisfactory, as ways that open the doors of human freedom and enable him to be his genuine self.

It is the counselor who enables the client to realize this renewal of spirit. In the therapeutic situation the counselor by his responses indicates to the client that all of his manifestations of freedom are acceptable. The counselor does not show approval, because approval does not contribute to the client's feeling of freedom. Approval and acceptance differ greatly: approval tends to build up defenses, while acceptance tends to build up personal freedom. The person who acts in order to receive approval unconsciously adopts habits that are substitutes for reality. These are the mental dynamisms, devices to guarantee approval, not his own ideas. Acceptance is not a response to what a person *does*, but what *he is*. The acceptance the counselor shows to the client is not a mark of approval or disapproval of his expressed feelings; it is a "positive regard" for the client as a person regardless of how he feels or thinks. It is in this situation of being accepted without a mask that the client gets the feel of living without it and realizes the sheer ecstasy of being his true self without sham.

The human person relates most effectively in his own reality, whatever that may be. His greatest potential can never be realized behind a screen but only in the full light of his own being-ness. But through rejection and deprivation of love he has assumed mannerisms and habits not for self-expression, but created to draw approval. But he cannot relate sincerely to others through these adaptations because he does not himself believe in them, and he represses his motives, knowing they are false. In this way he forms a whole network of behavioral patterns that in the end are ineffective because they have been built on false pretenses, on someone else's ideas. Buried in his unconscious these hidden defenses cause turmoil and his true self is covered over by patterns of defenses. The counselor, in communicating his acceptance and understanding by his whole being, by his presence, offers the client full opportunity to divest himself of veneers that conceal his true effective self, and enables him to act and choose freely.

In therapy, the client's defenses come to awareness, and for the first time he perceives their inutility. As his need for approval recedes, his emotional intensity lessens and his intellectual insight clarifies. At the moment when he realizes that he receives recognition as a person without these defenses, he commences to abandon them. The client comes to understand his potentialities and to assume responsibility for them; he faces them, evaluates them, chooses a means for directing them. In the presence of the counselor, the client thus becomes more and more able to distinguish between his own feelings and make-believe rituals resulting from accumulated repressions. With the help of the counselor's empathy also opens a wider spread of potential freedom. Gradually the client's estrangement lessens and in his continued relating with the counselor he gains a sense of being-in-the-world. As his relationship with the counselor grows, he becomes more able to extend this being-in-the-world to others. For the first time he perceives others and initiates genuine communication with them.

We have been describing the different methods the human person uses in trying to relate to others. A child's being-in-the-world is based on his emotional development and he relates to others accordingly. His self-identity is weak and he can participate only in a limited fashion. The child's world is filled with objects and things and he naturally uses them in his relationship with others. A client's emotional need may be compared to those of the child—but he is destined to live in an adult milieu and he meets resentment and prejudices when he attempts to relate far below the range of adult functioning. Adults expect egotism in a child, but not in an adult, even though his needs may be parallel to those of the child. In the counseling session, the skillful counselor is attuned to the client's emotional capacity and receives his infantile communications with continued warmth and acceptance. The client experiences, perhaps for the first time, the affectionate return of human response, instead of the hostile reproaches from those who do not understand.

PERSONAL GROWTH THROUGH COUNSELING

In continuing sessions, repeated experiences of fruitful human contacts enable the client to emerge from his immature thinking and to move forward with self-assurance. The time required for growth varies and many therapeutic sessions may be required for any noticeable change. Steady progress will depend on the client's cooperation and the counselor's skill, and upon favorable circumstances. Interruptions, avoidable or otherwise, tend to retard growth. But the climb toward maturity is gradual and requires time and patience. Later, the client, increasing in self-awareness, may leave behind the child's mode of relating and adopt means more akin to those of the adolescent. How *much* later will depend on the impoverishment he has suffered and the severity of his regressions. The counselor's insight into these many nuances of feeling help him to see the cues of growth, to know the client's subjectivity, and to respond at the level he understands best. The counselor's sensitivity to the client's realm of feeling and his system of communicating is the key to his therapeutic skill.

What we must realize about the changes in therapy is the internal renewal. Possibly the client's external world remains the same but he changes within. From his former experiences of rejection or deficiencies in basic affectional needs, he felt condemned and overwhelmed by the weight of his aloneness. The frustration and hostility within him grew and took on such proportions that they invaded his thinking and living. The resulting anguish of this pervasive dread had no specific object but filled his consciousness, and the client felt that whatever he did would increase his pain. Caught in the ambivalence between preventing further anxiety by reducing his responsibilities and thus removing himself more and more from others, and the fear of more rejection resulting from further attempts, he had been caught in his own confusion. Through the presence and continued warmth of the therapist, the client's awareness slowly emerges. In his gradual awakening, the release from anxiety animates him and he feels less compelled by unknown inner forces. It is this awareness of not being pushed by inner anguish to do this or that, and the liberation from coercion that pours balm on his wounds and restores him to health.

In his internal freedom the client regains a healthy vigor of mind and the energy to relate to others. Freed from disabling distress, his interest in the outside world increases and he looks outward for exchange, moving toward participation. In therapy the conflicts do not simply disappear, but by accepting himself and recognizing his feelings in clear awareness the client finds they no longer hold the same threat. The client in realizing his feelings learns to direct them. He is no longer subjected to the paralyzing agony of unknown compulsion, but can direct his dynamic energies as he chooses, utilizing them in accordance with his own values. As his inner freedom increases, his selfhood gains strength in its own identity, and he enjoys the feeling of power in regulating his affairs and guiding his destiny. The client can face his feelings, know them for what they are, and conduct himself in accordance with his dignity as a free person.

The changes in personality that result from these inner releases, though not sudden, are still remarkable. Because of the self-confidence he has gained, he feels able to relate to others, to move outward and begin the process of becoming a person-in-the-world. He enjoys others, is not afraid to meet them, no longer sees increased pain in each meeting, but rather an occasion for rich experience. The movement changes from sorrow to joy, from fear to courage, and from hate to love. What before was the source of crying pain may become the challenge of a forward leap into reality. The dynamic energies gain power as they expand themselves outward instead of remaining within, stirring unrest and spreading confusion. They find direction in achieving goals, following purposes, reaching for meaningful, valuable attainments.

In general, people choose to relax with friends whom they enjoy and with whom they are at ease. They prefer to exchange confidences with people who understand them no matter what their sporadic feelings may be. When one has to watch what he says, for fear of the other's misinterpretation, or guard his expressions for fear of being convicted or rejected, he is in hostile territory. In the workaday world of business relations and professional meetings, each one is aware of status and prestige factors. One selects his words, suppresses feelings of resistance or negative reactions, and follows a course of relating externally which may not be in accord with personal feelings. This is the ordinary procedure in groups formed on the basis of business interests or professional demands. But in these situations, the persons involved are not always completely themselves; often they play a role and adopt certain mannerisms of speech and action which for pragmatic purposes they deem necessary.

When the same people are relating to friends, they are different, more open, more natural, unrestricted by social formalities. The emotionally disturbed person, the neurotic person, lives entirely by a set of protective structures that are not formalities but are defensive devices and serve no real purpose. He has formed these behavioral patterns without awareness. He does not realize that his safeguards are appendages. The resistance against them that he feels within causes him distress because it threatens his existence. He doesn't comprehend these structures as unnecessary, nor does he realize that they compel him and do not serve him. He does not know that the internal resistance can be known, faced, and accepted without annihilating him. In therapy, the client slowly achieves this self-knowledge, dispels his fears, clarifies his feelings. He begins to relate sincerely to others in different capacities. He learns to distinguish acquired observances from internal convictions, to meet the demands of a situation without hiding his own uniqueness and to be himself without pretenses when relating personally to other human beings.

In being accepting, the counselor communicates his trust in the client, and perceiving this confidence in his person, the client's abilities fructify. The human person cannot be creative unless someone believes in him; he cannot grow in self-assurance unless he knows trust. As social beings, we are interdependent. We can enhance the existence of another or destroy it; we can enrich another or deprive him; we can facilitate his progress toward maturity or retard it. The human person possesses the potential for internal freedom, but he is also contingent and as a social being cannot reach fullness without others. He is not determined but interdependent and becomes more productive through the assistance of others. The human person enjoys achievements only when he can share them with others who are interested. No attainment or possession is selected purely for itself. For again, these are *things*, and for a person, things alone are secondary and provide no true satisfaction. Only in some dimension of relatedness does success exist. There is no human goal which stands completely isolated from the rest of mankind. Whatever gain, fulfillment, or victory man seeks is inevitably linked with the life and destiny of others. This is the essential contingency of the human person; his dilemma arises from the need to be free in the midst of his dependency. In the light of these considerations, the value of confidence and trust is more fully appreciated. The client, in sensing the profound trust of the therapist, realizes a surge of energy pulsing through him, bringing new vigor, and yielding fruitful results.

Presence of the Counselor

The presence of the counselor which the client enjoys in the counseling sessions reaffirms his identity. With time, this identity increases. The presence of the counselor transcends temporality, for it continues with the client after counseling sessions and eventually melds into his future becoming. As the effects of this immediate and recurring presence increase, the client's stability takes root, and his selfhood matures. The more solid his personal integration, the more flexible his personality. The stronger his sense of identity becomes, and the more self-assurance he has as a unique human person, the more able the client is to extend himself in a variety of ways. Flexibility in relatedness and the ability to orient to individual differences are marks of a mature personality. The genuine person, firm in his selfhood, develops a personality that is responsive to various problems of human exchange. In the presence of the counselor the client begins to see that self-isolation is not freedom, and that exchanging with another human person does not mean relinquishing independence. He grasps the significance of his personal freedom and his contingency.

Through the counseling process, the growing relationship between counselor and client is the phenomenon that effects personality changes for the client. Through this growth, he gains the self-sufficiency he lacked. By means of continual supportive attention, the counselor embraces the client in his own subjectivity. The client, during the sessions, rests "intentionally" within the counselor's being. Intuitively, the client perceives that his being resides in the intentional realm of the counselor. This being-in-another fills him with faith in otherness and, as he matures through these experiences, his whole being unites in an effort to receive another interiorly. The client then begins to attend to others. In a very natural developmental way his concentration moves outward, and he begins first to notice others, then becomes available for them. The growth of inner identity, his consciousness of his own individual self, rids the client of emptiness; he can give of himself because there is something within him to share. Where once he felt with agony that he was hollow and worthless, he now is aware of being a person with dignity. There is self-assurance in being this person, himself; he can freely offer himself to another. The client learns to listen to others with attention, to be aware of their needs and to be present for them.

Subjective growth and dynamic integration are achieved finally only through love. Deprived of love, the human person suffers misery and desolation. Surrounded by all material necessities, existing in the midst of humanity, immersed in crowds of people, he stands helplessly starved and alone without recourse to human love. The most poignant mental anguish, pain, despair, and dread that tears the inner being of the individual person, inevitably can be traced to a deficient love, a broken love, or the absence of love. No human person can exist in the fullness of being, unless he can love and be loved. Love gives harmony to the rhythmic flow of life and unites thought and action; it removes facades and reveals the beauty of presence and inwardness. It quiets internal turmoil and dispels confusion. Love synthesizes words and deeds, draws parts together, breathes wholeness and meaning into human existence.

THE COUNSELING EXPERIENCE

The suffering and distraught client needs a caring person to bring unity into his distorted thinking, to synchronize his unbalanced emotions. Incapable of reciprocating as person-to-person, he meets in the counselor the care and attention that affords him this opportunity. The concern the counselor extends to the client is not a commitment of friendship, but one of dedication. As a genuine person, the counselor sincerely commits himself to be for the client with a purpose that seeks his well-being. He uses his best resources to be of help to the client. By his presence in therapy, he offers himself to the client; by his attention he gives of his inner self, and by his acceptance and positive attitude, he receives the client who in his aloneness is as if bereaved. In order to heal the wounds and restore hope and freedom, the counselor's concern must be detached. In expecting no personal return, or mutual exchange, the counselor implies that his regard for the client is one of esteem, not demand. Beginning with the first interview, he introduces the client to a newfound freedom and for the first time the client knows existential newness and relief from pain and isolation. The care of the counselor for the client is real and sincere, but, is one of dedication, it maintains a relationship that will effectively permit the client to mature. It is not the mutual growth of friends that occurs here, but the mutual growth of counselor as counselor and client as client. This is essential to the very nature of the counseling relationship; otherwise its purpose is destroyed and it ceases to exist.

In the counseling session, the client experiences the unselfish concern of another, and unfolds in the warmth of this relationship. His personal unity, buried and latent, emerges to awaken a new life. The counselor's acceptance deepens as his knowledge of the client's subjectivity increases. With each forward movement, both client and counselor enhance the growth process. In this kind of mutuality, counseling progresses and achieves its aim. Only as a counselor can the therapist assist the client in his rejuvenation, help him to revive his atrophied psyche. If in the counseling session he ceases to be therapist, the client's progress is arrested. Thus in maintaining his position as counselor, his care remains unselfish and firm in its commitment to the client's fulfillment. For the counselor, it is the mutual growth of counselor as a person *for* another, and client as this being-in-the-world, that is important. Care and concern vary in expression according to their mode, but are nevertheless real in each of their enunciations. The care of existing for another as one ready to serve maintains the same reality as the care experienced in friendship. It differs in its existential nature but not in its genuineness. Sincere concern sees the potential of the entire person in his completeness, in his total becoming, and by its readiness encourages the self-actualization of the other.

The counselor extends himself to the client most authentically in his capacity as counselor, for that is his specific mode of caring for this person. Each form of caring includes essential aspects so that the care a man has for his brother is true but differs from the care he has for his son. For the client, the most important relationship is the mutual interchange in the counseling session, his opportunity to relate freely with another human person who cares for him as an individual endowed with dignity and worthy of respect.

In summary, the client's pain arises chiefly from the unsynchronized flow of his dynamic energies. At times he indicates a scintillating insight into his own problems, but despite this intuitive grasp of his own incongruity, is unable to emancipate himself. Before he can use his insight to advantage he must reduce his tensions. In therapy the counselor tries to understand how the client *feels* more than how he thinks. In emotional distress, ideas and judgments are not consistent, but fluctuate because of dynamic instability. The client may describe his problems; but he will also reveal himself in other ways. These ways may be more significant. His *manner* of relating events may be more meaningful than the events; his attitude may convey more than his words. The client lives in a world of feeling, and is governed by his subjectivity and consequently understands best whatever he absorbs on this level. The counseling process is essentially a communication of feeling, and nonverbal communications are more cogent than words. For the counselor it is essential to be able to respond effectively to both levels of expression, verbal and nonverbal. This is the key point of skill in counseling.

This is a brief outline of the process of therapy wherein the counselor, through his fullness of being as a human person, effects the growth of the client, soothes his pain, and draws him from his state of inertia into the living reality of being-in-the-world. By the counselor's presence, the client evolves from his constructed self-involvement through the various degrees of development until he reaches a mature personality. He becomes independent and enjoys self-actualization. Like a small child emerging from infancy, the child grows in the nearness of the counselor. This proximity of the other provides the necessary strength to initiate change. The counselor, by the strength of his own autonomy, and without condescension, without sacrifice to the dignity of the client's individuality, helps the client reach maturity. In the extension of his own person, by the intentional embrace of this suffering person, by the relatedness emanating from his own creative personality, the counselor leads the client to existential encounter.

In the words of Buber, the client ascends from his I-It existence to I-Thou awareness (Buber, 1958). In his new living he is ready for otherness and can relate on a subject-to-subject basis. At this moment the counseling relationship ends, for maturity seeks encounter with another, not in the capacity as a recipient client but in the full measure of reciprocal interchange, of mutual sharing and participation of one subject to another. The encounter achieved and experienced in the counseling relationship has become internalized by the client, is absorbed in his intentional knowing and renders him capable and ready for the encounter between himself as this mature person and another as subject. Personality, the effective personal relationship with others, in this way grows within the counseling situation. It is attained naturally through the course of living, exchanging with others on all levels of social development. In therapy, it is possible for the emotionally disturbed person to recover himself, discover his identity, realize personal freedom, and enjoy the fruits of effective living, as a being-in-the-world.

Counseling is a human relationship that grows and culminates in encounter. The reciprocal exchange begins with the client's need for help, a chance to gain freedom and self-direction. In his first attempt of self-expression, the counselor is another object in his world of things. Gradually, in the therapeutic situation, the client changes within, refashions himself, and matures in his own unique way.

Eventually, he knows and feels that he has become his own person and is no longer dependent upon the counselor as a recipient for his hostility and aggression. The client realizes that as an independent, mature person he can relate confidently to the counselor on an adult level. At this point counseling ends and the client is graced with readiness for encounters with others.

Chapter 9

DYNAMICS OF THE COUNSELING PROCESS

Counseling is essentially a meaningful reciprocal relationship between two persons by which the positive self-extension of the counselor enables the client to know, to become, and grow in selfhood.

Counseling is more than exercising techniques, the process of giving help to another, offfering services, giving advice, analyzing, or re-making. It is fundamentally a personal interchange between two human beings. It is interpersonal communication in focus; it is a relatedness that begins, grows, culminates in encounter. The counseling process varies in quality, extension, and success; but in its intensive meaningfulness, it is definitely a mutual relationship between two persons.

From this point of view, the aspects of counseling assume new dimensions and begin with attitudes differing from those that concentrate on the use of techniques. Many approaches in the counseling situation may be described as techniques, may be examined for effectiveness; but the entire setting in its reality is this particular exchange between two persons. The counselee who presents himself to the counselor is in distress, feels depressed and inadequate, desires to realize himself more as an effective human being. He wants to become and to be himself, not just to receive something from another. He needs the counselor's assistance and asks for it by his approach. He wants to be a subject, not an object of examination; he has already experienced this too much and he is in torment. Only by a genuine relationship with another can he become himself and through the counselor he hopes to attain this self-development. Even the patient who is too ill, too withdrawn, to approach a counselor is a person who is torn by his inner anguish and finally can be relieved only through human contact with another.

Interpersonal Relationship

The emphasis in a therapeutic situation must be placed on the nature of this human relationship, in the attitudes the counselor must have in order to be successful, on the condition that will create the best possible interchange between therapist and client. A counseling situation regarded as an interpersonal relationship, rather than the administration of therapy by the counselor to the client, will require distinct attitudes on the part of the counselor. This approach will differ in basic orientation from that of many classic theories. We must move away, even in our own thinking, from the idea of studying the client, analyzing his case, breaking him up into parts. And we must move toward the concept of the client as a distinct person in his experiencing, his suffering, his confusion, and distress. The shift is significantly one that involves a change of the counselor's consideration for the client as an object to be molded or changed, to the client as subject to be known and understood. This change of orientation requires a renewal of some attitudes and some renovations in theory regarding the exchanges between counselor and client.

In psychology, our first concepts of counseling evolved from the knowledge we acquired gradually through research, tests, and statistical analyses. We have benefited enormously from these accumulations of facts. In one sense these concrete data led us into abstractions and definitions so that we could classify and catalog the store of results obtained from scientific

observation. Personality itself has often been regarded as a structure and has been described in terms of numerical traits, sums
of characteristics, and the like. Personality disorders have been
divided into distinct groups, each with an orderly arrangement
of symptoms. All of these contributions classified the knowledge
obtained from observations which had been carefully studied.
This step has been a necessary preliminary for a systematic
comprehension of mental phenomena present in our cultural
patterns.

The research approach accentuates the knowledge of the
human person in terms of facts; the phenomenological approach accentuates the knowledge of the human person in
terms of his experiences and actions. In his intrinsic nature and
in his being-in-the-world, the human person is more a specific
being in action, than this being as a fact. The human person, to
be understood, must be known in his true dynamic nature. In
the counseling situation, the counselor must be aware of the client in his experiencing, know the depths of this subjectivity.
His knowledge of the client in terms of definitions, in terms of
"type," will be secondary.

If personality is the person in his relatedness to others,
rather than a structure composed of different levels, different
strata, then we must be concerned primarily with his problems
of relating to other people. Personality considered as a structure
is composed of parts. From a mechanistic viewpoint, the emotionally upset person is one who lacks stimulus-response efficiency, whose totality has become segmented. This consideration
is founded on mechanistic comparisons; man is analogous to a
machine composed of parts. When the machine does not operate well we look for some defective parts; or perhaps it has been
put together poorly, so we take it all apart and put it together
again so that the joints fit better.

This kind of analogy has influenced our relationships in
therapy more than we realize. There have been many concepts
that simulate a reconstruction of the personality, a rebuilding, so
that it will run more smoothly. When we pigeonhole a person as
a type, classify his characteristics, we begin with preconceived
ideas. And the results are sad if we have erred in the diagnosis
and reconstructed a pattern that did not fit. All of these notions
tend to regard the client as an object to be observed, evaluated,

rearranged. We try to fit him into some pattern or design which we vaguely conceive as "normal." The chief drawback here is that the client is in pain *because* he has already existed too long as an object, and has not reached the status of subject, or has lost this orientation. Our re-making him into another brand of object seems not to be the best solution. In the past, perhaps our failures have resulted from this misperception of the client. The successes may have occurred despite the misapprehension or, more likely, because the therapist in his actual therapy related in a person-to-person fashion, even though his descriptions may have been interpreted in mechanistic semantics. We have relied on the vocabulary of structure and of stimulus-response for so long we can hardly express ourselves otherwise.

UNIQUENESS OF THE CLIENT

Therapy, however, like other aspects of psychological knowledge, has evolved through many stages and is moving forward, becoming more secure in its own status. It has reached a level of prestige where it can afford to be more open and less confined to the regions of structure. We will always need scientific methods to ascertain global results, and the value of research need not be overlooked. But what is necessary is that we honestly appraise what is performed for the sake of research and what is evaluated in terms of the individual and his immediate personal needs. This individual, not just groups or samples of the population, is the client. If we are completely honest in this evaluation, our vision will be sharper, and we will grasp more profoundly the meaning of therapy for this person, and not for science or for all mankind. Therapists need a broad scope of experience, knowledge of facts, and a penetrating perception of human nature on a large scale. The client has other needs, but not necessarily this kind of knowledge. Ideational equipment will not assist the therapist unless it helps him to relate better to the client. Only then will it mutually benefit both. The therapist's knowledge of facts alone will not lessen the client's suffering; in the end only his effective personal relationship will alleviate the patient's distress.

In our highly structured society we all tend to build up

guidelines we do not believe. There are many systems that we cooperatively agree are necessary for good order and happy living. We want traffic laws so we can arrive at our destination in safety. We uphold restrictions that guarantee our rights and protect the common good. But in other more particular ways we establish facades no one enjoys but that we take for granted. But somehow everyone puts up with them and they continue. Commercialisms establish many little monotonous exchanges that no one seems able to forgo. Unconsciously we have absorbed much of this machinelike robot living into our mentality. In the roar of machines and the speed of rockets, we have lost á certain sensibility for the art of living, and are paying the toll by the steady increase in mental illness.

ALIENATION

In the very midst of this whirl we must be silent, reflect, and realize that the human being cannot be identified with the mechanisms and structures that surround us. In terms of selfhood and self-realization, structures are less important than relatedness; objects can never be substituted for persons nor things for people, nor elements for feelings. Our image of prestige and success is enmeshed in concepts of size and speed. In general, we tend to estimate the worth of a university by its numerical enrollment, the importance of a car by its size and speed, the significance of any organization, city, or industry by its population. Quantities are signposts of greatness. Our consciousness cannot help but be influenced by these environmental factors. Though we live in these confines, our own nature is very different and this is the crux of living for modern man. He has come to feel at home with terms that pertain more to his environment than to himself; he knows his milieu better than himself. He feels competent and skillful in repairing a machine, but lost when he must reflect on his own internal adequacy. He is a stranger to himself. Severed from outside props, he is unable to sustain himself because he does not know how. His potentials are there but often unrealized. When mechanisms, either objective or subjective, fail him, he is overwhelmed and feels that his world is closing in upon him. He wanders in darkness, aimless and benumbed by anxiety.

The above are a few of the general reflections that will help us to penetrate the significance of our being-in-the-world, and the adjustment required between our subjective selves and our objective environment. We cannot ignore either, nor can we interpret one in terms of the other. The person must relate to others and to things, but the problems of personality are always essentially based on difficulties in interpersonal relationships.

Relating proportionately to things, to environmental circumstances, is dependent upon one's satisfaction in human interchange. Dynamic growth depends on personal relationship and not on material acquisitions. A man is never so alone as he is when he resides in the middle of fame and fortune without another to share them. This is desolation at its nadir.

We must, therefore, strive to evaluate our thinking in the counseling situation and understand what it really consists of and what we hope to accomplish in the counseling process. For example, it is important to understand the being-ness of the client in the fullest context of that notion: our thinking in terms of person, our grasp of anguish and what it means, and further, what a-person-in-anguish means. Who is a therapist and what does he do during counseling sessions? The relationship between counselor and counselee will be the most important influence on the outcome of the therapy and the growth of the client. The nature and the quality of beneficial and therapeutic relationships is essential knowledge, and yet the most difficult to grasp and describe. In looking at counseling objectively, we are confronted with these distinct facets; and yet, in the reality of counseling, all merge into the flow of a movement and a dynamic process with no delineated characteristics. Semantics are quite inadequate to portray vividly the profound activity that occurs in counseling. Most counselors have become frustrated in trying to answer the questions of unreceptive parents or unsympathetic colleagues who say—"But what do you do in that hour, what do you say?"

We tend, in describing our activities, to think in terms of *doing* something, or *saying* something. We are unfamiliar with the very nature of being a person, or being-for-another. We are so dependent on speech and activity that we often forget the sources from which they arise, the basic thinking, the being-ness that gives them meaning. The subjective nature of our inner selves is difficult to know and comprehend because it is essentially intangible, in ceaseless motion and hard to grasp; it is nevertheless real and powerful in its existential worth.

The professional counselor knows well the indirect influence a good situation exerts on the counseling process. Though it is not the most necessary item, it is worth consideration. Our familiarity with the concrete will help us to recognize the most favorable setting. The extrinsic physical environment can be helpful in providing a conducive atmosphere. The more emotionally disturbed a person is, the more likely he is to attach symbolic meanings to simple objects, and the more sensitive he is to environmental atmosphere. As times goes on, a client who improves will be less affected by the physical surroundings.

ANGUISH

To know the client, we must know him primarily as a unique person in the profundity of his humanness. He is not a schizophrene or a neurotic; he is a particular human person suffering in the depths of his being, struggling with dynamic conflicts. No matter how he may manifest his suffering, whether by compulsions, delusions, or in less specific ways, one thing is certain in regard to each client: he is a person in anguish, who in his misery is reaching out to another. This is the basic unmistakable concept. It is often difficult to know specifically how he expresses his confusion, whether he has sought refuge in withdrawal, whether he is consumed with anxiety, or whether he is overcome by a mixture of both. These are secondary to the undisputable fact that he is a person experiencing pain. The client will reveal himself as he unfolds, and later he will describe his experiences. These are extrinsic to him and may be helpful, but not unless we first comprehend this person in his distress. Knowing *him* as a suffering person is more important than knowing *about* him.

The human person can never completely escape mental pain, but the poignancy varies from one person to the other. The client is enduring misery that has engulfed him and the intensity is great. Anguish in itself is a subjective experience no matter what its cause. It is not the physical suffering we know in a toothache or in a sharp abdominal pain. Physical suffering is an experience outside of our innermost self; it can be localized and described and often relieved with direct remedies. Anguish is intrinsic suffering. It lies in the nucleus of self and disturbs the centeredness of self. It is haunting and pervasive and hangs over everything else like a pall. It is inescapable for long and unendurable for long.

Herein lies the confusion and the desperation that accompanies it. Delusions or dynamisms of various kinds are last-resort antidotes. They are not adequate solutions but are often inevitable results. Anguish casts a shadow on every outlook from within the self. Sometimes the client considers real solutions, but anguish darkens the prospects with failure or doom. Anguish is often pure blackness with paralyzing effects. The intensity envelops the whole self and the light of reason cannot penetrate it. Under the spell of anguish, a person may be unable to move mentally in any direction and remains in a state of blind muteness, unable to see a way out and unable to hear consolation. He is desolate in the weight of the darkness that oppresses him. This is anguish in its most diffused form, a generalized mental agony. The client is always a person who is experiencing this kind of pain to some degree or another. This is in Kierkegaard's title-phrase, the "sickness unto death" which the emotionally disturbed person experiences.

Along with this endurance of general anguish, he feels alone—intensely alone—deserted and surviving on fragile ground with an unbridgeable gap between himself and others. Aloneness is anguish perceived in reflection. The anguished person as he sees himself in aloneness shudders, feels intensely helpless in his isolation, and experiences a burning desire to move out of the spot to which he is confined. He feels threatening tides in every direction but sees no way to cross the barriers. All otherness appears out of reach. Otherness lies in the beyond and gradually is slipping further away. Somehow he has been cut off, become an island in his uniqueness, and has lost hold of the otherness he once knew.

The more he reflects, the sharper the agony of aloneness. He wants to get back in touch, to be on the mainland, and be warmed by another's recognition. Aloneness is intensified by each reflected attempt to find the way back toward otherness. A misstep may widen the breach instead of bridging it. Past failures have already wrought enough havoc, and there is always the danger that a new attempt will end in failure. But the struggle between remaining alone, and the pain of possible failure in a misdirected move, mounts, and gains momentum. There is so much within that cannot be communicated lest it drive others further into the distance. What cannot be comprehended entirely cannot be communicated well; what is not communicated well can be misunderstood; what is misunderstood brings more aloneness. It is better not to risk communication. Aloneness is better than more aloneness through rejection. But there is that certain persistent gnawing that reminds one of the continual inevitable recession.

OTHERNESS

To endure otherness is painful because one sees the widening, but to turn around and gaze into an abyss, and perhaps realize nothingness, is excruciating. It is better to close one's eyes and not see; but if the eyes are closed at this point, how would there ever be enough courage to open them again, lest the otherness be out of sight entirely? It is best to look, but not see too much, when the inner awareness is clearer and the uneasiness of self-estrangement more acute. Is the self that is seen there the true self, or is it a strange self, different from what it was taught to be, unrecognizable? There is the searing pain of aloneness with oneself; to reflect and not find the self, but rather some kind of substitute, unknown, unfamiliar. (Kiergegaard, trans. 1941) Even *within* there is a gap, and the self is out of reach of self. This is the separation that shakes the very isolation and leaves no ground to stand on. Loneliness becomes immersed in the feeling of loss and separation, loss of identity, separateness from self. There is nowhere to reach, all is darkness and aloneness, stillness and muteness. The client who is emotionally upset to either minor or major degrees is beset by the feeling of being deserted, alone, and helpless.

Feelings of Confusion

Closely allied to anguish and loneliness is a feeling of confusion which the client experiences from conflicting emotions and frustrations. Emotionally disturbed people do not follow the path of reason because it is too obscured by their own feelings. They become entrapped in a vicious circle in trying to escape loneliness and, in doing so, they become more alone. They communicate their insecurity to others who, in turn, often shun them as unstable or unpredictable; confusion results.

People who have reflected on subjective experiences in intense emotions of fear or anger have described the inner feeling as a "blurred" sensation. Evidently the wave of emotion can reach a peak which tends to be more diffusive than penetrating. In any case, the confusion a client describes includes a blurred feeling, but it is different again from that experienced in an isolated incident of intense emotion. The blur of confusion results from a mixture of emotions, a state of being torn by many conflicting and equally strong feelings that are pulling against one another. The whole self is enveloped in a thick fog of ideas that do not coincide, and emotions that arise and fall spasmodically. There is no visible direction, no clear path, and the client gropes his way through, hoping to find some signpost or cue to a way out of the enveloping cloud. But the road behind as well as the road ahead is obscured. Direction of any kind is hidden in uncertainty.

Confusion closes off relatedness because it clouds the whole outside world and there are no clear-cut desires or aversions. Inner feelings are blocked and move in vertical directions rather than outward. Frustration results. Confusion brings about a mental nausea because functioning is impaired. The whole self becomes surfeited with a melee of mixed ideas, faulty judgments, and illogical reasonings. This hovers and clings without alleviation or transitions. Confusion sometimes becomes suffocating and chokes responses before they are formulated. The pervading density makes simple tasks difficult and arduous. Since the emotionally disturbed person cannot distinguish one thing at a time, the weight of duties and responsibilities becomes insupportable as he confronts all in one undetermined mass. The values and purposes once sufficient seem useless, and bewilderment follows the upheaval of these roots.

When ideals and goals are shallow they are easily upset by new situations which disclose their inadequacies. But the struggle in shifting to different guides is impossible if the new directions are not well defined. Indefinite conflicting principles and ideals create internal chaos and the person fumbles from one plan to another. He does not understand the old secure ideas. Neither the old nor the new suffices, and the middle space between them is a vacuum. One cannot breathe. To search for new guideposts would be a relief but the client is immobilized by the conflict. He is unable to change directions since he sees none, knows none. His predicament is increased when he realizes that his fixed position is not balanced or centered but lopsided and tottering. He cannot operate and feels lost in his blind alley. He is imperiled by all the outside forces behind the screen and feels he could collide head-on with them at any moment. He feels all kinds of irrational movements within him but cannot pin them down or identify them. They are *there*, milling around, but taking no definite shape, remaining amorphous threats which could destroy his toppling self. His whole being feels on the verge of collapse from the exhausting turmoil.

Confusion of great intensity crushes the person with the sense of being trapped. He feels like a victim caught in a net from which he cannot extricate himself. Something ensnared him unawares and he is unsure of how it happened. Vaporous blinders simply rose out of nothing and wrapped him, and his efforts to remove them are in vain. Just what occurred to cause the bedlam is unknown and he cannot remember exactly when he was not so afflicted. His misery appears without beginning or end; always there, on the increase, mounting to unbearable heights, becoming more impenetrable.

Confusion is linked with the agonies of indecision. Thoughts of selecting or choosing aggravate the uncertainties. For some clients certainties are minimal, and for the seriously disturbed they do not exist. The nature of doubt itself is suspension of judgment, which means the end result could be either one thing or another, or nothing. The constant swaying from one to the other, following the swing of the pendulum with an endless stare is the seasickness of the soul. There is no malady that yearns more for death, and is further from it, than the sickness from motion. Never fatal, never ending, when each movement is an eternity, yet a disorder which reduces man to prostration. Doubt leaves no freedom. Stripped of choice, man loses his true human dignity and remains on a vegetative level. He moves with the wind and bends back and forth without stability.

PATHOLOGICAL DOUBT

Uncontrolled doubt is the most disabling of all the conditions of the mentally disturbed, but is not completely separated from the others. When doubt prevails there is also anguish and confusion, but in its opposition to freedom it becomes a more difficult problem. Freedom unexercised leads to doubt, and the emotionally disturbed person has been limited in freedom for a long period of time. In doubt one idea cancels another, one value balances with an opposite, and the persistence of this contradiction leads to an inner void. Nothing within remains on a firm basis. The whole self is suspended in space with no relatedness. One cannot relate to uncertainty, because it implies a possible nothingness in either direction. The dynamic energies within stand in opposition to one another and are expended uselessly in debating one another. The self in its various experiences is overcome by a feeling of worthlessness, aloneness, emptiness, is surrounded by a meaningless world. When one's whole being is drained by doubt, nothing remains.

These nagging feelings of doubt that dominate the client are not merely intellectual doubts. They are often less definite, less attached to certain ideas, and more permeating. They infiltrate the minutest details of living; knowing is dubious and feelings are intense but undefined. The client suffers acutely, but is not sure whether he is angry or fearful, whether he has lost love from others or hates others. His quandary is incessant and invades his thinking and acting. The doubtful person hesitates over everything. He may continue suffering in this dilemma over each minute detail. Even if his conflicts are related only to major issues, his hesitancy is painful, for he is never able to perform without the residuals of doubt. He indulges in a constant pushing and pulling and, no matter what he does in the end, he doubts its value and worth. Each action performed in doubt makes the next one seem more formidable, and he hates his own potential for freedom. His indecisiveness becomes his only escape and dominates his existence. His only effort to relate is to clutch his own indecisiveness and in this one respect he is obdurate.

Pathological doubt seeks many kinds of refuges from indecision. Patterns of rigidity are often havens of protection, and wherever doubt prevails, rigidity reigns. Doubt builds and constructs protective devices of all kinds, none of which is enduring, but lasts only for a short time. Reality is meaningless because it requires risks, decision, and more risks. Reality is full of pain and must be avoided. This avoiding can be done by continued doubt. What is uncertain may not exist; and one does not make decisions about nothing. When doubts cease, decisions begin, and the pain of decision is worse than the pain of doubt.

The client teeter-totters back and forth, maintaining the meaninglessness and inutility of his own self. Dynamic energies are exploited in this up and down cycle. In this constant aimless movement, the self diminishes and is more threatened by the loss of equilibrium. The client loses a sense of direction and feels homeless; restlessness wards off reflection but offers no solution. The doubter flounders in a life that is purposeless and goalless, and his inner cohesiveness breaks in this inevitable confrontation with reality.

Prolonged intensity of emotions occludes intellectual insight and gives rise to doubts. When the level of intensity is reduced, the pathological skeptic regains his powers of discernment and choice. Old ingrained habits of indecision are less pliant and will show improvement only when tensions are relieved.

The emotionally disturbed person also expresses his doubts

through feelings of guilt. As the struggles with indecision continue, hostility and frustration ascend, dominate, and flow out through feelngs of guilt. The scrupulous person who is torn by feelings of guilt is reacting against the necessity of choice and decision. Scrupulosity evades responsibility, and hides behind symbols and ceremonials that offer temporary relief. Ritualistic behavior is substituted for decisions and the client sheds responsibility by meaningless gestures. In his symbolistic world, handwashing removes guilt; evasion, repetitive acts, and highly routinized behavior supplant volition. The scrupulous client forces others to tell him what to do, to shoulder the responsibility for his actions. He does not want to be accountable, for he cannot face the pain it entails. He doubts the validity of his own actions and foists the consequences on others whom he also doubts. His cycle of activities is relentless and fruitless. In his unreality the scrupulous person attaches guilt to meaningless trivialities, centers his living around them while his concern for actual values is minimal. He fills his world with senseless details in order to avoid reality, which requires obligations and the possibility of true guilt.

REMORSE

Deep within psychic areas of most emotionally upset persons is the torment of remorse and regret. These sufferings are not necessarily attached to moral problems. It is rather the experience of burning aches within that we refer to here. Mental sufferings vary in certain distinct qualitative ways. For example, loneliness is painful, but differs qualitatively from regret. Loneliness implies a certain sense of loss, of separation. Regret, on the other hand, implies a certain interior sharpness, bitterness, and a burning sensation. There are distinct differences among mental sufferings, and some are generally more tolerable than others. In Sartre's drama, *No Exit*, the character Garein calls hell "other people" (Sartre, 1960). A more apt description would be that hell is remorse or regret. Of all the interior sufferings, the one which is potentially the most consuming is regret. The attribute of despair, or irrevocability implied by regret heightens the agony. Other kinds of internal anguish do not include the same implication. Despair is a form of hopelessness, and includes a generalized state experienced only by some severely disturbed individuals. But every emotionally disturbed person endures a certain amount of remorse. This is despair attached to a specific problem or to an event. Remorse may not be consciously experienced but may be intermingled in the confusion and anguish pervading the self. However, the presence of remorse in each upset person, and the qualitative experience which this means for him, must be recognized.

Remorse keeps anguish alive; it smolders deep within and from time to time erupts into flaming sheets. The client is suffused with compunction he feels but cannot identify. It binds him to whatever is negative in the past, constricts him to his problems without any hope of solution. Remorse has inbreeding effects and tends to reproduce itself, to accumulate. It often remains latent, but undermines positive attempts to free oneself from the past. Each new thrust of forwardness rebounds and is crushed by regrets that are reminders of former failures and the possibility of others in the future. In ruminating over the past, the self is so concerned with remorse that it becomes petrified, as thoughts of future repetition pass through consciousness. Even the happiness and success of the past is erased by the searing pains of remorse. It is only the stifling effects of past misfortunes that well up to blot out interest in the future.

All of these negative and debilitating mental experiences that cloud the client's mind deplete his strength. He feels drained of energy and resources and is helpless. Because his dynamic energies are functioning powerfully in a negative direction he is unable to progress. He feels as if he is being pulled and dragged away from the lifeline that he holds. His helplessness is the result of the ambivalence resulting from his constriction of the past and his dread of the future. The present finds him treading water and getting nowhere; he struggles merely to survive.

MENTAL SUFFERING

From these qualitative descriptions of mental suffering we can appreciate the needs of the client who comes to the counselor. Each person will differ decidedly in the degree of mental disturbance that he endures; each client will have adopted certain habits and patterns of activities to express his distress. In the process of therapy the counselor perceives these. But the most important consideration is the client's suffering. No matter what particular mode he assumes, he suffers; he is in pain and he comes to be relieved. This is the primary claim, and all others must be relegated to the background. Even the normal person who is experiencing an acute emotional distress will consciously or unconsciously be suffering from anguish, confusion, loneliness, doubt, regret, and helplessness. The intensity of his conflicts, however, will not be as severe as that of the neurotic or psychotic; but comprises the same basic elements of psychic tension.

The neurotic patient develops certain emphases, and resorts to complicated physical or mental designs; but the same fundamental experiences are present to a greater degree. The psychotic is often seriously disoriented, much more removed from reality than the neurotic; but his condition results from a combination of the same intrinsic qualities of mental pain. Whatever bizarre pattern he assumes, the patient is essentially a human person in this mental agony, unable to be himself, unable to become, or to enjoy another. This is the core of all human distress, whether it is just an overshadowing nuance in normalcy, or whether it has reached the blackness of psychotic oblivion.

The euphoric manic is just as lonely as the withdrawn schizophrene, though he manifests it differently. The schizophrene may know more acute loneliness and the manic-depressive more intense despair, but both will experience some of each. Neurotic and psychotic patients are in anguish and conflict just as is the normal emotionally upset person, only many degrees "more so." The existential reality of the client is his suffering, his pain not his symptoms. A focus on the symptoms first is putting the cart before the horse. If it were possible to relieve the psychotic (whether schizophrene or manic-depressive) of his anguish, his confusion, his loneliness, his remorse, his emptiness, his symptoms would disappear. He would shed all of the defenses he has constructed as a refuge from the pain he cannot face.

It is true that the process of therapy must reach into the self to remedy the deficits that accounts for the suffering. These will differ in quality, intensity or proportions, but the fact remains that the basic suffering is more important than the particular symptoms. Symptoms and types are secondary. Accurate knowledge of the symptoms does not guarantee awareness of this person in his suffering. One must know him in his uniqueness to understand his pains and the syndromes he has adopted. It is the person himself who is primary in counseling, not his malady. The emphasis on the person in his suffering will shed more light on the relationship of his symbolic reactions to his total world of experience. The counselor will understand the symptoms better in knowing the patient. In studying the symptoms first, the therapist may lose sight of the patient, and the patient may feel exploited as an object of observation and study, instead of recognized as a feeling person who wants to be known and accepted.

In discussing the various dynamic movements underlying the classical categories of mental disorders, we have attempted to offer descriptions to help us leave the textbook and enter into the client's existential experiences. For in his realm these symptoms have a very different context. Textbooks and lectures give us ideas about symptoms, ideas about feelings, but do not convey feelings. The client's anguish is a feeling, not an idea about a feeling. The intentional nature of feeling is more difficult to grasp than the intentional nature of ideas or judgments. The existential reality of the client is intentional anguish, i.e., the anguish he feels through the dynamic energies that move within him. Even his ideas about feelings are not the feelings themselves. His dynamic experiences, in a sense, are more internal to him than the ideas he forms about them. For example, choosing and deciding are more interior than knowing and perceiving. One can choose one idea in preference to another, so that in this one sense the idea is "outside" the movement of selecting. Comprehension of the intentional inwardness of dynamic propensities brings us closer to the psychic pain, the confusion, the helplessness, the client experiences within the core of his ego. His outward manifestations are but reflections of this inner reality.

Each human person knows his own subjectivity by reflection. It is true that the subjective experiences of one person can never be identical with those of another; but what is the same is the nature of subjectivity. Knowing our own subjectivity helps us to know that of another. Through him we can further grasp some of the particular qualities unique to him. We cannot penetrate this existential reality of another without trying to put aside the techniques designed for investigations of concrete movements. In the case of the client, his symptomatic behavior, the odd gestures, the distorted speech, are all concrete and lend themselves to more objective evaluation. But the subjective quality of pain and anguish that these symbols represent cannot be reached with objective tests, and cannot be alleviated by an objective approach alone. More is necessary, namely, awareness and entrance into the feeling world, a listening to the pulse of the psychic pain that fills the existential realm of the distressed client.

Deprived of affection, confined to an undesirable milieu where freedom is denied, the human person will decrease in his ability to relate effectively. The strong, mature person can weather rejection and adversity better than one who has not reached fullness of being. But no human person can exercise his capabilities or continue in his actualization if he is deprived of mutual interchange for a long period of time. Personality effectiveness continues and increases with the opportunities for self-expression. Divested of possibilities for positive exchange, the personality diminishes.

The client in his anguish and confusion is unable to discern the source of his problems. He is bewildered by the pain that envelopes him and does not see what he can do to better his circumstances. He cannot distinguish between the cause and effects of his problems because his emotional intensity blurs his thinking. He feels intensely but cannot think clearly. The desire to relate to another human being is his most crucial need but he does not know how or where to begin. The only possible permanent relief he can receive is acceptance and understanding from another person. No other remedy will suffice to lessen his anguish. Most medications give only temporary relief or lessen the sharp edges but do not seem to offer permanent alleviation. Often, removal of the medicines intensifies the original anguish, makes it more unbearable than before.

The suffering experienced in anguish, loneliness, and confusion, by its very nature is psychological, subjective, and concerned more with the inner self than the needs of the body. It is a phenomenon known to all. It is inevitable in every life but not necessarily crippling, as in the case of a neurotic or psychotic. It is real; no one will deny its existence and its nonphysical nature. It cannot be localized like a physical pain but in so many ways is more acute, more distressing. The whole self is more concerned with anguish than with bodily pain. There is some satisfaction in the realization that physical pain has a certain spatial quality— that one can say it is here, or in this region. But when the whole self, body and mind, is suffused with pain, gripped by a relent- less, subjective throbbing, the person reaches a "standstill." He cannot extend himself to others, he can only remain helpless and inert while the anguish strengthens and mounts higher.

Understanding the effects of the dynamic experiences that fill the life of a person in emotional distress, whether his condi- tion is temporary or serious, we can see that the root of the prob- lem is in the area of interpersonal relationship. The client has reached a state wherein his personality is not functioning well. He cannot enjoy another's world. His own domain is too torn by strife and struggle to permit time or energy for another; yet, he is dependent on another for relief. He cannot exercise the very activity that would bring him solace. His suffering is the separa- tion from otherness, yet he cannot reach out toward another. His alleviation rests in otherness, but he cannot receive it. Only through otherness can he regain his own freedom, but he can- not recognize the signs that indicate the outward route. His most immediate need is the experience of another accepting him without expecting return, understanding him without test or trial, receiving him as a human person without demanding an equal regard. Above all, the client's primary need is the ex- perience of relief by the presence of another, the realization through contact with otherness that there is hope. The actual feeling of another's complete interest, another's being-ness, is the first awakening to the recovery that can be achieved.

Chapter 10

ENCOUNTER IN COUNSELING

The word encounter needs clarification, for in ordinary parlance it often follows its root meaning which infers a conflict, as in a battle or a duel. This connotation brings to mind a certain hostility or opposition characterized by resistance and counteraction. The use of the word for our purposes will follow a more phenomenological bent and refers to a certain kind of positive relationship between two human beings. In an ontological sense, two beings oppose each other as two separate identities in the world of being. The one is never the other, and is always completely segregated from the other by the individuality of his being. In this elementary ontological sense, encounter refers to two-ness and describes a separateness in existence, a distinctness, one being differing from the other. In this sense there is a certain "opposition." For a relationship to exist there must be two beings, otherwise there is complete unity and oneness. In our consideration of personality, the word encounter will refer more specifically to a particular kind of relationship that exists between two human beings.

SUBJECTIVITY

As in the various developments in this particular study, our purpose is to take note of the subjective nature of human experiences, especially as they are related to personality. As we have mentioned before, the values of objective measurement are numerous. But there is something ridiculous about empirical studies trying to explain the real nature of human relationships as they exist for each in his own subjectivity. The minute array of calculated stimuli-response activities attempting to account for the meeting of minds, the quality of dynamic experiences, leave a certain void or vacuum. What does all this really tell us of the inner dimensions known so vividly? These experiences say volumes more than numbers and percentages can ever reveal.

For example, the internal experiences accompanying a single pleasant conversation become different phenomena when explained in formulas and mathematical hypotheses. We can measure the intensities of physiological functions in different emotional reactions by a polygraph and we can see the results on the data sheets. We can measure endocrine secretions, heartbeat, blood pressure, etc. All of these recorded data together do not suffice to indicate the qualitative experiences known and felt within the person himself. In the world of being, experiencing is far removed from the registration of these effects on a machine. The "message" has little meaning for the person when he reads it, accurately recorded, in numerical symbols. The entire qualitative reality of subjective knowing and feeling is lost, and there is a certain pitiful abyss between these two spheres of subjective experiencing and objective measurement. The whole inner self and its world of meaning sees all these measures as strangers, fragments of a whole, torn from the center and lying as meaningless shapes and forms on a table of blocks and buttons.

Somewhere there lies a reconciliation beween these two dichotomous viewpoints, between these two modes of knowing and being. It is not the sphere of numerical infinity we meet in the person, but rather a world of being encompassing another realm, over and above symbols alone. The person's world is one of response, interchange, of giving and receiving; it is a dynamic world rather than a world of stationary emblems. A person is not always at this point in space, but rather a being in space, yet communicating beyond it. A deeper knowledge of our intentional nature, how it relates to the order of measurement, how it transcends it, should draw out some unified significance. Measurement without qualitative description substitutes only a diagram for the pulsating, knowing, feeling, human being, for this person as he lives in the fullness of his inner and outer being.

THE MEANING OF ENCOUNTER

Encounter, then, refers here to whatever we can distinguish in the intentional, subjective world of the individual as he relates in a specific way to another. There are many kinds of relatedness; one passes by many people in the busy street, and a superficial relatedness occurs. Then one relates more definitely as one speaks to one person or another, asking for directions, entering a store, making a purchase. One meets many colleagues at a conference, at a dinner; a person dines with many different people, speaks with many throughout the days and months. There are many interchanges with children, parents, friends, relatives, associates. Every moment of existence includes a relatedness of some kind, direct or indirect, immediate or remote. Some forms have more depth and extension than others, some have long duration, others are fleeting and vague. All leave an impression on the inner being and form a part of the experiential world of relating.

Encounter is more than all of these and yet includes elements of each. Encounter is an experience of knowing, in the fullest sense of the word, the being-ness of another person. This knowing by its very nature includes a reciprocal knowing. The actual encounter itself is intentional in nature and includes a strong subjective experience as well as the direct awareness of the other person's separate existence. It is the intentional existence of this other within me that accounts for the uniqueness of encounter. The other person exists in objective reality. The mode of his existence within me, i.e., my knowing him, is an *intentional mode* of existence. All that I know of him exists within me, but my intentional knowing can reach different degrees of profoundness. My exchange with another includes a mutual giving and receiving of a subjective nature, yet I recognize that this person with whom I communicate is totally outside my individual being.

Encounter may be accompanied by physical exchanges; by a handshake between friends, by sexual relations between married persons, by simple gestures in other situations calling for a physical response, such as in times of grief, sorrow, joy, elation, excitement. However, these physical aspects are accompaniments to encounter and not part of its essence. Encounter can exist with or without these particular expressions. Yet, encounter is not merely a platonic exchange of ideas. It is the experience of reciprocal entrance into the subjective worlds of each other. Words are media but even words take on a different meaning when the presence, one to the other, is actualized in encounter. It is an effortless process, because the attention is drawn rather than forced and the other's subjectivity seems familiar, already known, rather than another world far removed from one's own. There is a certain at-homeness in the other's subjectivity, i.e., in his mentality, his inner perceptual world. There is an at-easeness in his reciprocal awareness of my inner thoughts and this gives rise to a mutual interflow of exchange that is free from anxiety or fear of being possessed.

Encounter is fundamentally free and unhampered. It is devoid of tension and joyful in being accepted, received, and understood. Free interchange is the keynote here and this freedom also includes the ability to retain ideas and feelings or express them without fear of another's reaction or resistance. Precision and care in external verbalizing is unnecessary since understanding and acceptance precedes all. Words make no barriers, because presence is understood with or without them.

PRESENCE

Encounter pertains to *being* rather than to *doing*, even though activity or interchange may follow. Being someone— being this one, individual being—for another, forms the core of encounter. I am for this person and he is for me. Because I am this being for him, he can be what he wants, and I can be what I want without destroying encounter. Encounter exists with or without words, enveloped in time, but timeless in its duration; surrounded by space but limitless in its form. The silence of encounter can be just as meaningful as a verbalized dialogue. Two people may enjoy a reciprocal presence, pursuing different tasks, without words, yet with a deep awareness of one another. It is the free interchange of subjectivity, freely given, freely received, that constitutes this kind of personal relatedness.

Actual presence will enhance interchange, but absence will not alter the relationship. Actual encounter recommences at each meeting whenever time or space interferes with the direct experiencing. For the actual reciprocity continues, whether actual presence is realized or not; encounter is a relationship of being-for-someone more than merely with someone. Even if I am with the other I do not experience encounter if I am not for him by my presence. Being with someone is accompaniment, co-existing along with him; being *for* someone is existing and consciously being-for-him because he is this particular person. I can be with someone, day after day, working at his side and never exist for him nor he exist for me. With-ness in itself is meaningless as far as exchange is concerned. Human, personal interchange depends specifically on an interpenetration of two subjective worlds where the inner egos form, reside, and become.

Knowing is not simply seeing the external man, his physique, his gestures, listening to his words. Knowing is entering into his thoughts, which are accessible because he makes them so, freely opens his awareness to my ideas and feelings. In common parlance we say, "we are on the same wave-length"; the message he sends out from his subjective world is received by me because I am attuned to his "station." Otherwise all that he says filtrates the air and is lost.

Another example: When one must stop and think, "I must be careful in regard to what I say, lest he misinterpret my meanings or my motives"—the distance from encounter is great. The relationship in this case is a fearful one, and feelings must be disguised and ideas must be dressed up to make a good impression. There is a false ring to such relatedness, a hollowness that resounds from within. The only result is a dent in another's consciousness, an impress on his subjectivity; one becomes a fragmented image in the memory of another, or a "thing" to be considered, not a person to be encountered.

Subject-Object Relationships

Too many circumstances and habits in modern living have developed this kind of subject-object relationship between human beings. By this is meant that a meeting between two people, often for purposes of business, commerce, transactions of all kinds, results in a situation wherein each looks upon the other as an object, or a means to an end. The manager interviews a man for a job. He examines him not from the standpoint of a human person, his personal values, his goals in life, his inner dispositions, but first and foremost for his usefulness. How will this man serve the company, how efficient will he be for our business; in other words, what kind of an object or cog will be in our structure. This is looking upon another human being as a "thing," stripping him down to see if he can fit into this frame; in so doing he depersonalizes the man.

Modern living is immersed in this kind of existence. Persons who spend most of their waking moments in considerations of this kind will inevitably develop habits of regarding human beings as things, objects, tools, mechanical instruments. This distortion of thinking, this process of depersonalizing others, impedes facility of real communication. This frame of mind will be hard to change, and communication with all persons will tend to become a subject-object relationship. The same manager in his capacity as father or husband will find the subjective reorientation in his own family more difficult. Unconsciously he may carry over this subject-object method of relating into his own family circles and may fail in his capacity as husband and father. He may tend to treat his children as numbers or as things and ignore the value of their true being-ness. In this way the family unity disintegrates and the personal exchanges between father and family become automatized.

To avoid these catastrophes, the businessman, the boss, the manager, must seek ways and means of reinforcing his own human commitment so that his preoccupations with the necessities of his job do not replace his personal relationships within his own home. Our technological society has imposed many similar obligations upon man that deprive him of opportunities to meet his fellow man on a person-to-person basis. More and more it has alienated him from the personal group living so essential to his nature.

In the universities and schools where learning, by its nature, depends much on effective communication, mass education has created problems that could defeat the purpose of education. So often the question arises: How can it be that in our society, where education is more accessible than ever before, men are less educated in the true meaning of that word? A reevaluation of what "education" for the masses actually implies will reveal many presently unobserved features. This kind of education does not always achieve its own proposed goal, namely to enable a man to know truth more clearly and to live more richly a life of human fulfillment.

Some individuals may experience encounter only late in life because of circumstances or retarded personality growth. Until one has realized himself as subject he will be incapable of entering into an encounter with another. For in each relationship he will always be seeking the satisfaction of needs, and will relate to others in such a way as to accomplish this. Not all human relationships involve encounter; but what is important in all human relationships is the self-integration of each person, enabling him to be a subject when this befits the situation.

For if he has not reached his full stature as a subject in himself, and in regard to others, he will not be able to relate proportionately on any level of human interchange. His relatedness with others will always take some form of self-fulfillment, rather than an awareness of the other in his capacity as this unique human person. The permanence of any human relationship depends on the maturity of the persons involved. Persons who relate to each other because of neurotic needs will eventually sever their relationships. If one person relates to another because of circumstances, or merely by means of talking, complaining, criticizing, eventually his relatedness will collapse. When the circumstances are changed, the relationship will dissolve; sooner or later a relationship based on superficial exchange will likewise vanish.

PERSONAL UNIQUENESS

Encounter is further characterized by intuitive insight into the other's uniqueness. Uniqueness is difficult to grasp because of its singularity and because no exact standard measures it. A certain quality enhances and individualizes every particular human person. Not only by his individual essence is he unique, but also by the particular way all of these attributes move together and unite to form him as this person. The external differences we observe are numerous and complicated, but the nuances within the subjective world of this person are limitless. Uniqueness stems from a unified subjectivity expressed through external patterns of communication. This total reality distinguishes this person from all others. To perceive this in another fully, or even partially, requires profound knowing because the perception or uniqueness is not the simple awareness of an object; it is the combined movement of intellectual apprehension and dynamic possession of the good that is herein revealed.

Encounter is rarely, if ever, a result of a moment's consideration or a fleeting awareness; it is a consummation that arrives when maturity of personality is achieved. It begins with human exchanges through ideas, interests, or experiences, of which encounter is the culmination. It is not a physical attraction that may be desultory, fluctuating, coming and going, varying greatly in intensity. Encounter grows into a strength that is beyond the limits of the physical or purely emotional levels. All of these human aspects are fibers of encounter; but it is the mutual appreciation and acceptance of the uniqueness that is the basis of encounter. The physical and emotional aspects alone are too vacillating to form the core of encounter, but are important when they are proportioned to the persons and the situation and enhance the relationship. Moving in harmony with the mutual pursuit of the good of each person, they merge into the whole experience of encounter. The dynamic flux is the animating power within encounter, but follows knowing and appreciation. In encounter, one relates to another with his whole integrated self, *for* the other, for his good, and the other returns all reciprocally. For example, if certain physical aspects are in accord with the situation, are harmonious with the good of the other, then they enter into encounter because they belong to this relationship. But, if they do not accomplish the good of the other, even though they satisfy, they do not enrich encounter, but rather tend to destroy it.

In summary, we see that the basis of encounter is a subject-to-subject relationship, and its essence is the mutual appreciation of individual uniqueness. Uniqueness, in turn, is the particular unity of the subjective and objective qualities that is the oneness of the person. The awareness of this totality of another brings joy and contentment to the perceiver. It is not a joy that is sought, but a result of the appreciation realized. One cannot always appreciate what he knows in another; perhaps he does not see what is really there, or is blinded by his own deficiencies. But the fact remains that one does not and cannot appreciate every human person in his totality. This is beyond the limits of one's extension and belongs to a Being greater than the human person. No individual is capable of extending himself to all in this particular manner. He does not have the capacity to comprehend fully each uniqueness, but his actual experience of encounter with one person will of its very nature enhance all of his relationships and interpersonal communication with other persons.

Encounter with one person does not separate a man from all others or lessen his exchanges with them. These effects occur only when he tries to possess another for himself or when he is possessed by another as an object. These conditions reduce his ability to communicate well with others, to relate, and to be with others. When a person, in this way, becomes an object to another, he loses his freedom and this loss alienates him from other persons. He is not free when he is curtailed by another's possessiveness. Encounter is characterized by freedom from self. Freedom belongs to each individual in his capacity as subject in his own realm and befits him as a human person with his incommunicable right to fullness of being.

Intuitive Insights

Intuitive insight into another's subjectivity follows the usual steps in abstraction and understanding required for the formation of ideas, judgments, reasonings. It includes the direction of all this cognitive power toward another's interiority, plus a simultaneous dynamic reception of what is seen and understood. The intuitive insight of encounter is the subjective assimilation of knowing, feeling, and willing in regard to another, and is the result of a positive regard for the uniqueness comprehended. Enhanced by the reciprocal knowing and accepting of encounter, this intuitive insight will also be keener and more profound in other areas. The capacity for knowing, appreciating, evaluating other persons, situations, and values will be considerably expanded. Encounter leads to more openness to truth, to goodness, to beauty in all of its forms. The energies within tend toward a strengthening synthesis which enables a person to function fully, to experience fully, and to be himself as a complete self-actualized person. His aesthetic awareness is greater and he is attuned to the richness of simple beauties which surround his life. His joy is increased and he is more expansive with others. His whole being, integrated by the fusion of all levels, moves in the flow of its dynamic power, progressively, smoothly, harmoniously, and achieves, produces, forms, creates. Encounter sharpens self-awareness; and through the other, one comes to know new facets of his own subjectivity. He realizes new potentialities within his own being which he can share through charity and love with many others. His work and achievements abound with spontaneous sharing and produce creative effects in others.

Intuitive insight is closely akin to a scintillating awareness of intellectual nuances and a keen sense of humor. We speak of a sense of humor and realize how greatly this power differs in degree and extension among human persons. A sense of humor requires insight into essences because it is the awareness of incongruities that gives rise to laughter. But the apprehension of the incongruous will depend on the sharp awareness of what is congruous, and this is derived directly from one's knowledge of essences, one's ability to discriminate between essentials and attributes. A keen sense of humor depends on this intellectual grasp of incongruities and is effortless and spontaneous. Two persons who enjoy the same kind and depth of humor, who have similar capacities to grasp the many interrelationships that cause humorous events are closely allied in their modes of thinking and evaluating. We are usually sympathetic toward others who make us laugh with them. In encounter, a wide difference between two people in this kind of intuition would be rare. Humor itself is not essential to encounter, but the same perception of it indicates the capacity of each to enjoy mutual intuitive insights for other dimensions of relatedness.

While the beginnings of encounter may develop by an exchange of ideas in a limited area, they will not reach a standstill at this point. The exchange, the reciprocal awareness of new knowledge, will be extended into more personal affairs, family life, sorrows, joys, burdens, interests, ideals, and goals. The sharing is spontaneous, deepens, and leads to mutual enterprises and undertakings. These include other people and at the same time foster growth in encounter. The mutual exchange of encounter is beneficial to both. It stimulates better performances in professional tasks, happier family living, and opens up new interests. Whether the other is present or not, the work and achievements of both are enhanced by the knowledge that all can be shared, received, and understood. The encounter, in its mature depth is pervaded by a unified response of knowing and feeling, giving and receiving; the existential experiencing of each is powerful and enduring and fosters a state of well-being.

INWARD VISION

Many human relationships lack a recognition of inwardness. We see external actions of others as isolated movements because we identify these with the person himself, missing entirely the inner reality they symbolize, or perhaps not knowing what they symbolize. To know the external person is to know very little of his real self; yet, so often the whole man is described, judged, evaluated in terms of these superficial expressions. Insight into uniqueness sees the consistence in these relationships between the outward expressions and the inner reality. For in each individual a relevancy and meaningfulness exists between the objective expression and the inner world. This is the essence of an authentic person. The eyes of hate or prejudice will be blind to this uniqueness, for they can never discover the reality within. The illuminations of discernment are occluded by hate and by the barriers of denial. Intuition, insight, understanding are dependent on the enlightenment of intellectual processes. Dynamic pressures, especially those of negative emotions, tend to diminish the cues, and reduce the clarity of the data from which abstractions are made. Only persons who are open to otherness, free from habitual emotional domination and negative obstructions, will be capable of encounter with another. Encounter is achieved through an open system of readiness to receive, spontaneity to give, a largesse d'esprit, and an aptness for appreciation, for valuing otherness for itself.

Encounter is knowing another in his completeness. Knowing is loving. The knowing of encounter is the kind of radiant insight that penetrates the inner man and sees the ontological goodness that lies within him. Knowing, understanding the good that is in this unique person, is followed by loving what is known. The love of encounter embraces the good, seeks to enhance the worth of the person, to-be-for-him so that he may increase in his becoming. The very act of loving encounter is also reciprocated freely so that the good is exchanged and both are enriched by their mutual beingness. Encounter is an unveiling of hidden potential, of latent qualities, of unknown dimensions. "Letting-a-person-be" opens the inner light of his personality (Heidegger, 1949). The warmth radiates and gives effervescence to his spontaneity. Within the deepest recesses of each human person there is a potential for natural elegance and charm. Encounter actualizes the dignity within and reveals hidden qualities.

This is encounter in its fullest sense. The degrees of knowing that precede it may be many or few, of long or short duration. These are the contingencies of situations and of the individualities concerned. Encounter, then, is achieved through maturity of personality. It enables a person to relate fully and beneficially to others. This capacity includes at the same time a person's power to receive, to absorb, to become in the light of what he has assimilated from another. The fully developed personality will increase, move forward in a state of continual becoming, because each meeting with the other will occasion new facets, new dimensions, revelations of many diversities. Even if no other actual meetings are possible, the individual himself will continue in this process of growth. Encounter accomplishes a permanency of the inner self and enables it to remain *one* in its integration, but *continuous* in its becoming. Encounter is living love, is charity in its existential reality and authenticity. It is not confined to one experience, and in its deepest form cannot be realized in every association. Each encounter will enhance the other, because each reinforces individual growth and personal maturity. Encounter enriches human dignity, makes a person more capable of being himself.

A true encounter increases the selflessness in his regard for others in different relationships. The professor who has experienced encounter with his colleague should be a better husband, a more mature father, because of his growth as a person. Likewise, a husband who has encounter with his wife will be a more mature person in his other interpersonal relationships with colleagues, associates, and particularly as a father to his children. A marrige that is not enhanced by encounter becomes merely an association between two human beings, and will be prone to terminate or continue in a haphazard fashion. If it is not graced by encounter it lacks strength and spontaneity, and the concurrent relationships of each partner suffer proportionately. Marriage without encounter is an immature relationship. For encounter in marriage is the union of two selfless loves joined together in this particular relationship for the purpose of mutual assistance in seeking each other's good. In this selfless pursuit lies the joy and nobility of the marriage encounter.

Every human life has the need for many different types of social relationships for its fullness of being. Lesser types of interchange gradually grow into more profound affinities. The considerations of child development and adolescent evolvement demonstrate the slow, gradual unfolding of more temporary forms of relationships. These are essential to childhood and adolescence; they are the beginning stages of social awareness, and in these stages only the initial forms of relatedness can occur. But when they do take place and proportional responses are received, the child continues in his social growth, and as he develops, becomes the adolescent who in this preadult life must pass through further phases of formation. In the socializing process, time is not the measure of maturity, as in the fixed chronological order. The movement toward social maturity may require a much longer duration, for the achievement of effective interpersonal relations and of a full personality will be reached only when the person has become integrated sufficiently to-be-for-another, and for others.

THE FOUNDATIONS OF ENCOUNTER

Only the mature personality, as we have indicated, can experience true encounter. Everyone, even a child, must experience it in some form or other; if he does not, he will not know the essence of love. The child receives love and must absorb much and reciprocate, even in a limited way. The adolescent, in turn, requires much more love than he is able to return; his own growth needs are too demanding and he can only share in half-measures. His ego strength is undeveloped and he instinctively strives to build it, to reassure his inner self with little concern for the needs of others. Gradually, as his ego knits together, he becomes aware of others for themselves. He must receive mature love in order to become mature. He depends on parents, teachers, counselors, for continued support and love and with their aid, little by little, becomes the adult he hopes to be. His knowing is greater than his capacity for self-formation. He perceives in others what he wants to achieve, but is dependent on their love to reach this attainment. He cannot reciprocate as adults can. He must be loved deeply for himself in order to experience what love really is, to know selfless love, and how to extend it to others. He loves himself primarily until he is secure, and when his ego strength is solid he seeks to love another. If he has never known real love from another he will not be able to love selflessly; he will not be able to realize encounter as an adult. The adolescent who is deprived of selfless love from his parents, who has never received a valid substitute for parental love, never experienced a real friendship or helpful counseling, will inevitably become a sociopath, a person incapable of extending himself to others.

Many adolescents, because of these deprivations, move from one activity to another, in heightened agitation and restlessness, seeking desperately to fulfill themselves. Unstabilized by lack of real love from others, they look for it blindly in all directions. They often indulge in sexual excesses, and try to fill the gap with physical satisfactions that only increase their deeper needs. Their sexual escapades often become driving forces that obsess their thinking and impede their growth or even cause regression. Adolescents follow many paths, sometimes frantically, in trying to build the ego within them so threatened by disintegration. The need to grow socially, as well as physically, is fundamental to the human being, and one's happiness as a person depends on progress in this direction. As the adolescent fulfills his own needs, his awareness turns towards others and he is ready for the risk of encounter. The adolescent who moves toward the apex of his growth will have already known the mature love of others, and this experience enables him, as a young adult, to perceive uniqueness in another.

DEVELOPMENTAL LEVELS OF COMMUNICATION

Communication, no matter how minimal, includes a risk—the risk of conveying something not entirely intended. Communication is always a sharing of one's being with another. Since it is always through some medium that a person must convey the being-ness of himself, there is the possibility of misunderstanding. In the everyday world, there is the continual round of daily activities, involving superficial interchanges. These are routine duties, routine exchanges, never completely separated from the individualities concerned, but for the most part skimming the surfaces. This give and take is habitual, without conscious concern. It is the deeper relating that involves the greater risk, and the degrees of risk are proportional to the degrees of relating.

When a person attempts to communicate something of his real self, he takes a real risk. He must again resort to some medium, and always with the chance that the medium will fail him, or he will manipulate it to his disadvantage. He may fail to communicate his real intentions, his true self in this situation. He also takes the risk that the person to whom he is communicating is at the moment closed to his offer. Perhaps that person is overcome with fatigue, preoccupied with problems, hampered by obsessive thoughts, concerned with his own projects, and consequently is not receptive to any communication. This is the outcome he must always hazard. Another person's disposition and preconceived notions may also misconstrue the content of his communication. He may want to communicate himself, and he may want to be receptive, but the obstacles and the risks he takes are many. Or he may want to share his feelings with another who is not receptive. In this situation the risk again is very great. All along the evolving social process the risk is there, and the ability of the child, adolescent, and adult to move outward often depends on the successes experienced in risking communication with another.

From the beginnings of infancy, as the child emerges into awareness and perceives others around him, he tests them. He pushes forward into this world of otherness with tiny steps and countless fumblings. He learns in rudimentary fashion that certain ways of communication are more satisfying than others. These early habits are significant to his later forms of communication. If he receives an abundance of comfort for his faintest whimper or show of hostility, he quickly associates these responses with his inner feelings and will try to use these methods to his advantage. Love received for more positive movements will help him to form positive habits.

The older child communicates in a more definite fashion and more precisely learns modes of relating that are worth the risk. He can endure more refusals and employs techniques to his advantage. His social needs are greater than those of the young child, but not as acute as those of the adolescent. However, he obtains greater satisfaction in achieving *with* others than he does without them. So he strives to communicate, particularly with his peers whom he meets in school and at play. He contends and competes with them and learns to share. But he learns first of all to share only *things*; even this kind of sharing he does with reluctance and difficulty. He lives and moves among things, but people are also the objects of his needs; he accepts them or rejects them according to those needs. In this elementary way he works with the fundamentals of exchange. Little by little he interiorizes the essentials of exchange, mostly on the basis of things. At the same time the selfless love he receives from his parents or other adults helps him to feel relations that are essentially personal. With his peers he learns fair exchange, but not love in the true sense. A child's capacity for giving of himself is very limited, because his integration is in the beginning process. But the social values of living and working in groups help the child to realize social standards outside of himself. As he interiorizes them they are transformed into attitudes and habits of acting.

The exchange of things continues with many nuances and merges into the deeper relationship formed in adolescence. But the adolescent moves beyond the realm of things; he is no longer satisfied with objects alone. His inner social sense knows other values and he perceives numerous subtleties in human relationships. He has experienced joy and sorrow, love and hate, anger and fear, courage and desire, often with great intensity. Feelings have become more valuable to him than things, but he still seeks or avoids experiences through the media of things. He has need of continued love without being able to return it, and is torn between the desire for independence and his crucial dependence on his parents. He cannot give to others what he demands from them; the anguish of this struggle is an adolescent crisis. The pain of the adolescent's struggle for maturity requires the continued understanding, but not indulgence, of parents and teachers lest he be crushed by the oppression and weight of his strife. The emergence of the self to an independent, integrated ego is a painful process, burdened with conflict but spurred on by the spontaneous resilience of youth.

The adolescent struggles are wholesome forms of growth and are essential preliminaries to complete attainment of adulthood. As an adult the adolescent must know the whole gamut of dynamic energies before he can synthesize them. He cannot direct his own energies if he does not know them. As he meets these inner contentions, faces them, evaluates them, selects and chooses, he becomes himself and is no longer dependent on the guidance of his parents. On the threshold of adulthood, "having" becomes "being." Moving steadily forward through the maze of mingled dynamics, the adolescent gradually extricates himself from confusion and in so doing gains self-assurance, a sense of completeness, and an identity he enjoys as his own.

Psychological identity has its origins in the essential nature of man. No other sensitivity within him is so intimate and so immersed in the substance of his being. Identity arises from the harmony of this inner being, from the unity of his dual nature, from the fullness of his diverse self, integrated into a whole person; from the completeness of his emerged ego, free in its self-direction. Metaphysically and epistemologically he is *something*. Metaphysically, he is a being, this being, this self. Epistemologically, he is this being with certitude. This philosophical awareness, direct or indirect, focal or marginal, has a profound effect on the individual and the persons, groups, and circumstances of his milieu. The conviction of his being this person is the course of his action, gives design to his motives, meaning to his purpose, and influences the patterns of his actions.

SELF-ENCOUNTER

Before he can be for someone else, before he can relate, experience encounter, he must first of all be someone, be this individual person called "I." Extension to another means extending that being. But first of all this self must exist in itself; it must be real, authentic, true, one, whole, and entire. The total self vibrates with action, with the need to give and to share, to become, to be for another and to let another become in the strength of his being-ness. There is no greater human agony than the interior groping to know oneself, no greater loneliness than to penetrate the inner marrow of this being, this self. This is the profound anguish that envelopes the self that is stranger to itself, and searches for the inner reality that can be recognized and understood as the true self. There are many for whom the challenge of knowing themselves is greater than they can meet. Terrified by the unknown inwardness, they relentlessly pursue whatever can distract them from this inner tension. They seize every opportunity to dissipate their energies. They multiply activities in meaningless proportions that only serve as a temporary escape from inner threats. Groundless fears drive them to seek others solely for the sake of company.

A person is often ill at ease with himself alone, and cannot read, study, or live without being in the immediate company of others. This is the psychological fear of nothingness, the fear of looking within and finding nothing, or of finding something other than what one wants to find. The human disparity between what one is and what one thinks he is may be too great for the conscious self to bear. There are many possible disparities that the person eventually must face in order to feel secure in himself, in order to reach a sense of identity. The differences between what he is and what he thinks he is, between what he is and what he thinks others believe him to be, are inevitable. In the unfolding of personality, these are the problems each individual must face for himself and by himself.

In the reach for identity there is always a time when the person, in his aloneness, separated from all others by his uniqueness, must look with eyes wide open at this nakedness of his being. It may be a moment of terror and will always be a moment of profound anguish, of total solitude. In this aloneness he must stretch across the darkness and reach for the light that comes if he accepts himself as this person. This is the essence of Tillich's "courage to be," the courage to be one's self rather than another, to accept one's self as he is, here and now (Tillich, 1952). In doing so the individual must also accept the inevitable disparities always existing between his inner subjective self and the way he expresses himself to others. The realization that the expression of oneself to another and to others is an art that requires skill is a process of becoming rather than a state of being. The person's inner being-ness will always be his own essence, namely, this individual, this self; his being-ness will always be the permanency to which he can adhere, an ontological reality that is his existence as this being.

He must also come to realize what his uniqueness is as this particular individual, what this "I" signifies in its unity of inner being and outer relatedness. For it is only in his relatedness that he becomes fully his experiential self. It is not sufficient for his being-in-the-world with other human beings to know only that he exists. He must also know and have some certainty in regard to how he exists for others. The human person in the root of his being is social, is concerned with others. He cannot live in the world of others and be totally indifferent to his surroundings, nor to other human beings. His knowing and feeling, his intimate self, depends on the world outside of himself and he can fulfill himself only through knowing others, feeling what he comes to know.

His whole being, then, is involved in relating himself to the world in which he exists. As soon as he enters into the world of others, from the first moment of birth, he begins to be-in-the-world. The search for identity begins. Identity is not a conviction reached with any degree of finality, and no state of euphoria offers a perfect synchronization between what one is and what he wants to be, what one is and what others think he is. This is the realm of dreams and reverie. In reality there is no absolute merging of the subjective and objective world; by their nature they are one. The becoming of an effective human being is a continuing process, evolving through many changes. Modifications reduce the disparity between the inner and outer world of self. The self can never be narrowed down to a combination of percentages, ranging from introversion to extroversion. The real, complete self is more than these symbolic inferences. But the realization of identity permits the human person to achieve, to expand himself, to grow by means of personal transformation and to enjoy encounter.

Chapter 11

THE INTEGRATED PERSON

Person—A Unity of Character, Personality, and Temperament

In the whole range of phenomenology, there are many levels of meaning and many regions of being. But the raison d'etre of this book is to unite the ontological meaning of person, the psychological meaning of personality and counseling, from a phenomenological point of view. In developing the concepts of counseling and personality, other areas of phenomenology are implied, but require a thorough discussion apart from our purpose. Inevitably existing within the human being are many interwoven factors: Moral, religious, spiritual, and physical aspects have specific objectives of their own and merit a complete presentation outside the scope of this study. By clarifying a few terms and introducing a few distinctions, this interpretation of counseling and personality may surmount some of the problems of reductionism, whether they be psychological or theological. In so doing it may reach a more realistic knowledge of the human personality as it pertains to the individual existing in his everyday living.

167

For example, anguish and dread are not necessarily the result of moral problems, but more often of a person's awareness of the gap between his real self and his idea of self. This disparity which confronts man in his self-awareness becomes a psychological problem rooted in his ontological being. We might even say that in this consciousness of himself, of what he really is and what he wants to be or aspires to be, he comes face to face with the awareness of his ontological existence. It is at this moment that man realizes his finitude and meets the problem of physical death. In these different orders of man's being the same problem exists, but is expressed according to its own realm.

Psychologically, man experiences aloneness and anguish when he feels apart from others, when he is unable to relate as he wants to, when he neither loves nor is loved to suit his capacity. Ontologically, man's existence is real but limited and contingent, endowed with freedom, and constricted by time. Spiritually, man seeks for self-extension and fulfillment beyond the confines of his personal disappointments in himself and in others, above the contingencies of his being and past the barriers of death, into the realm of an Absolute who can sustain him and bridge the gaps in all the domains of his being.

The concept of person is an ontological one and refers to man's essential nature and mode of existence. Various philosophers from Aristotle to the moderns have presented many different explanations of man as a person. But in his existential reality man is an individual, apart from all others because he is this person, with an indestructible identity, and with a dual commitment arising from the spiritual and human aspects of his substantial nature.

Character

The term "character" is more directly related to man's choices and decisions in the moral order. Many times a day the human person meets situations in which he must choose between good and evil, virtue and vice, better and best. With each of his choices he molds his character, strengthens or weakens his moral stamina. Motivational systems and personality patterns will influence choices and the formation of character. But personality in itself cannot be identified with character. A person's manner of relating to himself and to others may be attractive or not, may be constricted or expansive, but will have only an indirect influence on his decisions in regard to good and evil. Within each self the measure of maturity is the link that binds together character and personality; but it is man's substantial identity that is the core of unity in each individual as he expresses himself in moral choices or in his encounters. The mature person will be sufficiently free from inner constrictions to make decisions on his own, and this freedom, in turn, will enable him to develop character and to regard the rights of others. But the human person is endowed with both personality and character which coincide on the basis of selfhood and identity but relate to different modes of activities and different patterns of behavior within the same individual.

Temperament

"Temperament" refers to a person's reactions stemming from his particular physical structure. The ancient Greek philosophers related temperament to the humors of the body—and with some degree of truth. Some educators have used the word temperament in a very generalized way by lumping together physical, moral and so-called personality traits into one confused jargon. In reality, temperament is more directly related to man's physical constitution and to certain inherited physical dispositions than to other factors. But even in the more measurable areas of physical structure, categorizing specific "types" is an abstraction at best, since no individual is a pure type.

The investigations of Kretchmer (1926) are valuable studies, but provide no conclusive evidence for perfect types. Sheldon's (1954) comprehensive studies of bodily types have produced many interesting theoretical considerations, but have provided no basis for "personality types." What we do know from these and various other research works is that individuals differ in physical reactions depending on their bodily structure and physiological systems. Some individuals more than others react more quickly and spontaneously to certain stimuli. These reactions depend on synaptic formations within the nervous system. Given a stimulus, one person may respond quickly and strongly, while another's response to the same stimulus may be slower and less intense. The physical complexities are many, and the possible intensities of response and the time intervals will vary with each individual. Temperament refers more directly to a person's reaction potential than to personality, bodily build, or character.

Personality

Personality is related to each of these facets of human person, and yet it is distinct from each. The attempts to categorize personality have been numerous, and theories have been based on a substantial variety of factors, traits, temperament, etc. We may add all of these traits together and yet, as the gestaltists say, we find the *sum* of all the parts insufficient to describe the totality. This person whom I know, this personality I encounter, is experientially more profound than the most exact summation of traits and descriptions. It is easier to study personality from a theoretical viewpoint than to know an individual experientially. It is possible to investigate with skill and accuracy the various theoretical traits and structures of personality patterns and still not comprehend this individual personality I now encounter.

The self in its physical aspect (i.e., as a body), its relation to space, and all the exterior components that this involves, form certain constituents of personality. In terms of measurement, evaluation, and prediction, even physical aspects present difficult problems. Research on physical and mental traits, as well as on other personality constituents, offers valuable insights. But it is the self in its subjective, intentional world that presents the most significant problems, the most intricate processes.

Projective techniques have been helpful in studying and investigating subjective realms within the personality. A careful review of the complete tabulated results of a battery of projective tests, along with detailed information of a case study, presents an image of an individual person with a certain amount of accuracy. Yet, the image conveyed by the test results is different in extension and comprehension from the phenomenological reality one comes to know in an encounter with this personality. It is true that the tabulations are objective, and the processes of encounter are subjective.

But one cannot ignore this subjectivity that exists. Somehow it is there—real, potent. Paradoxically, to ignore this subjective area is to be unrealistic. Such "unreality" characterizes the "operational model." A whole world of space, time, phenomenological depth, is bypassed. Whatever dynamics can be known and expressed only through personal encounter must also contribute to our knowledge of human personality. Research cannot be confined to diagnostic techniques. Personality is an area open to many avenues of thought and study; it will be grasped more fully as it is considered in all of its dimensions.

Personality has formerly been considered as a structure composed of traits; this suffices to give an exterior description, but does not account for the intricacies of communication and exchange so essential to personality. In a trait theory, self-confidence is one of the fibers of the structure, like many others that make up the whole pattern.

Let us consider this trait as an example. In this structure of personality, what is self-confidence? Is it a segment or line that passes through a part of this individual? Is self-confidence something apart from this individual that can be put on at this moment like a coat, or left behind like a pair of shoes—something to be worn on certain occasions? Evidently self-confidence is more than a part or a property of this person. It is this person as he feels in regard to himself, and as he manifests this feeling for himself to others. It is not something which he can put on or take off. True, in certain circumstances this "trait" varies and can be observed in different degrees. But self-confidence as an intimate process within this individual being and immersed in his existence, has a deeper significance. In relation to others, through different media—e.g., language, gestures, expressions —self-confidence will vary, but not in its ultimate sense. The comprehension of the self in its interior realizations will vary greatly from a knowledge of the self in terms of traits. The understanding of another's self-confidence as he extends himself to others in this particular way will convey a very different significance than the knowledge of this person who has the trait of self-confidence. A world of difference lies between "he *has* self-confidence" and "he is self-confident."

As we survey the field of personality studies, it seems as if we have begun in the wrong direction. We have assembled groups of traits, designed them into tests—then, we have sought to fit in the persons who have been tested—clients, counselees, students, etc. We try to see how each one may be placed in this compilation. Is it not possible that there will be characteristics, shades, and nuances in the uniqueness of this individual that are not included in this particular series of tests? How will that be calculated if it appears? Somehow the ideas must be juggled around or reconstructed so that this person may be interpreted according to these designs. What one assumes is that this test, or this system of traits, is all-comprehensive.

Like the bands of the spectrum, or the color pyramid, this nuance of uniqueness must fall within the given range. When we work with parts and systems we are working within confined limits of lengths, widths, sizes, and shapes. The physical characteristics of the person fit fairly well into specified categories: weight, height, auditory strengths, visual capacities. But is it possible to devise a similar system for the human personality which emanates from his very being, forms an intimate part of his very existence? Can I calculate his communication to another, or even the qualitative degrees of his self-awareness? This brings us to a threshold different from the world of number, even the world of infinity and space which numerical concepts try to include, and back to personality as an individual's manner of relating to others. Personality refers to the unique way in which a person relates to himself, to others, to the world in which he lives.

The Integrated Self

An example will help us to understand the uniqueness of personality in its very beginnings. Craig was three years old, and at this early age, personality was beginning to stir in a definite direction. The uniqueness of Craig was disarming. In his presence, techniques of measurement, skills of personal communication, descriptive categories of three-year-olds, took on very nebulous dimensions. Craig was entirely different from the image which the compilation of tests provided. One counseling interview sufficed to indicate that he demanded complete and full attention. The more one searched for professional explanations, the more Craig disappeared from the picture. Once categories and percentiles were left behind, the world of Craig was more accessible and many facets of his uniqueness unfolded and led to valuable insights and helpful solutions.

Craig was upset and sometimes struck his baby sister forcefully. He was frequently disobedient and had shown fierce anger. He had bitten and scratched his mother, and injured his playmates. On the other hand he was highly intelligent, strong, and intuitive. He wanted nothing to do with tests or toys. He preferred to look, to listen, to remain quiet and pensive, but was not withdrawn or apathetic. Craig accepted the counselor's attempts "to be present" and also his attitudes of wanting to be of help. Soon afterwards, Craig was telling stories about a friend of his who feared and hated his dad and resented his mother's frequent absences. Many, many months later, the friend's name was dropped and Craig began to talk about *his* dad, *his* mother, and *his* sisters. Craig grew more loving and less fearful. One day he decided he would prefer to stay home and play with his sister, and be with his parents, rather than come to the clinic. Craig had arrived; he was past four years old now.

It would be more difficult to relate accurately the methods and procedures that helped to relieve Craig of his fears and anger. But his continued growth and adjustment indicate the deep changes that occurred and the growth that helped him to mature. Knowledge of techniques, long experiences with other children and adults were essential resources. But Craig's uniqueness defied all usual forms of testing or communication. Presence, acceptance, attention, in whatever ways they could be dynamically communicated in the language of a three-year-old, were the only assistance Craig would tolerate. Sometimes he wanted to sit quietly, to look around, or just "to be." It was best for the counselor to do the same. Craig was independent and wanted no gesture of affection. At other times he wanted to look at objects in the room and examine them. The counselor's silent undivided interest was essential at these times. Once he scribbled on paper and caught the counselor looking at the clock instead of the scribbling. He promptly terminated the session. During the following session, the counselor passed *his* test, namely gaining Craig's trust, and both Craig and the counselor continued to grow and mature.

The self is ever unique, and only through personal encounter do we come to know and to relate to a human person. We must be aware of the basic nature and universal properties unified and expressed in a style that is completely Craig or Michael or Marie. The counselor will be reinforced by his extensive knowledge of human nature, and the refined measures of scientific investigation. But he will arrive at a knowledge of this person when his extensive experience is combined with a personal awareness of this individual in his actual unfolding. If this approach is impractical in terms of knowing thousands and thousands of individuals then impractical it is. But if it is true, even though impractical for the population at large, it deserves recognition as a truth.

The eagerness of scientific research for objective data about large population samples has lost something of the real and true of the individual person. There is a reciprocal need to realize that, in knowing this individual, I do not know general trends or the statistics of a large population; when I know these statistics, and general group trends, I still do not know this person, this member of the group, in his fullness and in his existential reality. An encounter with a person will reveal significant factors that statistics fail to indicate. Statistics and personal encounter are not mutually exclusive; but the self, as such, can only be known through personal encounter.

Chapter 12

ORIGINS OF EXISTENTIAL COUNSELING AND PERSONALITY

Advances in psychological thought have initiated many inquiries concerning the human personality, its origin, nature, development and concepts of psychological maturity. Increased interest in mental health and in the growth of effective personality complement the rapid progress in counseling and psychotherapy. Modern research studies offer many explanations of the personality in terms of structure and traits. Experiments in social psychology, tests, and profile analyses have provided invaluable data for the investigation of group tendencies and cultural norms. These a posteriori approaches have designed operational models and proposed various interpretations. The results of these studies have been helpful in evaluating population trends and experimental data. We are better able to distinguish between counseling techniques for groups and those that are significant for the individual personality.

In the person-to-person encounter of the clinical or counseling session, and even in ordinary interpersonal relationships, the knowledge of personality structure in terms of traits has been helpful but not sufficient. Even the most careful analyses derived from the projective measures have not been sufficient means to guarantee effective counseling for another individual. Awareness of these inadequacies in knowing and helping others has prompted a search for other dimensions that should produce better communication. Knowledge of another in terms of structure, traits, diagnosis, does not suffice, nor does it necessarily enable one to enter his inner world. In the dynamic movements of the anguished person lies another dimension that is often impervious to description analysis. One grasps the multidimensional whole, perceives an entire self of another, only by entering into his subjectivity; this can be accomplished only by relating to the other, person to person. It is precisely in the relating process that these other subjective dimensions unfold.

In group measures, or even in individual tests, there will always be certain barriers to these inner domains that will open only through a meeting with the person himself. What I know about this person from a vast accumulation of accurate objective data will only be realized in fullness and in living reality when I know this other through personal communication. A whole world of dynamic movement as it exists in process comes into focus before me as I meet another, and this experience presents a new dimension in my understanding of him. My factual knowledge of him differs in quality. This meeting with another is the existential reality of knowing in its fullness; the rest is a knowing of facts, a knowing of another as an object, or a thing. To know and understand another as he exists in his full reality one must communicate with him, one must know something of his inner self "in process." This kind of knowing and understanding will vary greatly in extension and comprehension, and will depend on many personal factors within each individual concerned. For this reason, traits and measurements often seem sterile in the presence of the person himself, known in his total existential reality.

Two vast storehouses of human resources lie before us: the achievements of scientific studies of man in his environment and phenomenological studies of man's subjectivity. Modern man finds himself in a whirl of speed unknown before, pressured on all sides to produce more and more. Insatiable demands confront him in work, social living, and in his individual existence. Modern man lives in a more complex situation and to know him better as a person in this environment, we must devise new approaches. Even though scientific and phenomenological studies arise from opposite sources, there is no reason that they should cancel each other. On the contrary, with man as a common basis of interest, they should be complementary.

A complete grasp of the human person requires both sources of knowledge; he is neither solely his subjective ideas, nor is he merely his speech, gestures, or reflexes, molded by his environment. He is the unified totality of his inner and outer self and it is in this unity of his complete self that he exists and continues. In this self that "is," becomes, and moves toward another, lies a reality of being, substantial in itself and continuing in its extension; in this self lies a nature, partly subjective, partly objective, and it is in the struggle between this twofold commitment that man experiences his most profound anguish. To grasp the depth of this anguish, to reach into the depths of this twofold nature, we must know a person in his interior self and in his environmental social structure.

In medieval times, the study of man was more concerned with problems relating to his nature than to his personality. Philosophical interests centered around the essence of man, and the pivotal question was, "What am I?" Modern man is more likely to ask, "Who am I?" *What I am* is basically a question that pertains to my nature as a person. *Who I am* is related to concepts of self, my awareness of myself, and how I feel about this self and the world I live in. These concepts form the basis of counseling and personality. What I am and *who* I am are related and mutually influential. In one sense of the word we might say that *what* I am is more concerned with my essence as a personality and is therefore an "existential" emphasis. Personality, then, is an existential reality, none the less real because of its subjective implications, but unique and less capable of a concrete interpretation.

NEW DIMENSIONS OF THOUGHT

In phenomenological studies we find many emphases and interpretations that reveal subjective data and help us to grasp the inner world of the human person. In seeking to discover the uniqueness of an individual, one must pass through the barriers often found in exterior behavior. The purpose of our approach to the human person is not to abandon invaluable scientific research, but rather to continue in the process, go beyond into other realms not easily measured objectively. In the clinical and counseling situation, the psychologist is confronted with problems of anguish, of dread, of despair, and incalculable degrees of interior pain. His comprehensive knowledge of facts alone does not equip him to know a person in his anguish.

The clinician sometimes finds himself well versed in the theories and figures that refined research has revealed, but helpless in the presence of a client disoriented by pain and confusion. Somehow he must penetrate this maze of human complexities, and a certain reality within himself must reach out to the client, must be able to communicate relief, even without words. It is not only the exercise of his verbal techniques or his diagnostic skills which reach the inner world of the distressed client. The warmth and acceptance within his own unique being must accompany all the rest, and only through this medium will he actually be able to gain entrance into the inner self of the client, which harbors the anguish.

This, then, is the aim of the phenomenological approach: to distinguish between objective, structural analyses of the human person, and the subjective, dynamic flow which is this being-in-the-world, as he exists in himself and in his relationship to others. He exhibits many traits and characteristics in varying degrees: self-confidence, personal worth, antisocial habits, egotistic tendencies, nervous mannerisms, withdrawn mechanisms, ad infinitum. But these exhibitions do not reveal the qualitative dimensions of his inner domain, the depth of his feelings, the power of his choices. These exterior characteristics are the signposts indicating a direction or a cue but they describe nothing of the vastness and profundity found in the encounter. The whole inner dynamic system is complex, moving, changing, as it pulsates within the self.

But uniqueness and identity merge, and give continuity to the person. Despite the flow of processes, of movement and change, the person remains ever this one individual self with a definite relatedness to all others. He grows, becomes, and changes, but in the renewal retains his individuality. Because of this combination of stability in the midst of change, intercommunication is possible and interpersonal relationships become powerful, meaningful bonds, regardless of what the alterations may be. In the phenomenological approach to interpersonal relationships, what actually increases, deepens, and causes change is not the knowledge of personality traits an individual may acquire, but the growth of insight and awareness. By his awareness of others and their feelings, and through an ensuing facility of exchange, the human person grasps another's intensity, appreciates his poignancy, and is able to communicate in such a way that he reaches these inner needs. At times it is not so much what one says as how one says it that makes the difference in this kind of relating. Beyond diagnostics lies the challenge of crossing the threshold, entering into the world of this person and comprehending it, receiving it, and exchanging in such a way as to promote becoming and enrichment.

PHENOMENOLOGY OF PERSONALITY

In personality studies, the uniqueness of the individual has led to the consideration of this phenomenological approach. For the human person, individuality takes on special dimensions arising from his power of choice, decision, freedom, and ability to communicate reciprocally with others. In the psychology of personality and of behavior, these aspects have special significance and, for this reason, it is in the area of personality and counseling that phenomenological interpretations have aroused most interest. "If there is to be a science of personality at all it should do better than it has in the past with the feature of personality that is most outstanding—its manifest uniqueness of organization" (Allport, 1955, p. 21). This is what Allport calls the "dilemma of uniqueness" and is the unifying factor that has eluded the behavioristic and mechanistic approaches we have known so far. The phenomenological approach attempts to study this uniqueness, regardless of its intangible qualities and incalculable features.

This emphasis on man's uniqueness and the interest in his subjectivity arises from two main sources: first, clinical research has led to a reconsideration of many psychological theories of personality and counseling techniques. The great increase in mental disorders has created a special interest in preventive measures and an orientation of research toward the positive studies of integrated personalities. These factors have produced more insight into the uniqueness and dynamic systems that seem to transcend certain established laws of behavior. Secondly, the philosophy of phenomenology followed by modern existential theories has given impetus to the study of man's subjective life and has elucidated the inner dynamics of the human person. Behaviorism has contributed much to our knowledge of man's external behavior but has offered little to explain inner dynamics adequately. Physiological descriptions fail to account for the many meaningful qualitative nuances.

> Man lives in a radically new dimension of reality. He is immersed in the world of nature up to his neck, subject to all of its laws and forces. However, he has the capacities for self consciousness and meaningful use of symbols. These introduce a psychological freedom into his behavior that makes its explanation in reductionistic terms impossible. That is, although man is subject to the laws of physics, chemistry and biology, these laws do not account for all the phenomena of his existence. (Basescu, 1962, p. 149)

In philosophy, phenomenology is carefully differentiated from existential theories. In psychology, particularly in personality studies and in therapeutic situations, the word "phenomenological" is sometimes used in much the same sense as "existential." Both terms refer to an emphasis on the importance of man's inner reality and his subjective experiences. From the psychological viewpoint, Rollo May (1961) explains the difference in these two terms:

> . . . phenomenology, the first stage in the existential psychotherapeutic movement, has been a helpful breakthrough for many of us. Phenomenology is the endeavor to take the

phenomena as given. It is the disciplined effort to clear one's mind of the presuppositions that so often cause us to see in the patient only our own theories or the dogma of our own systems, the effort to experience instead the phenomena in their full reality as they present themselves. It is the attitude of openness and readiness to hear—aspects of the art of listening in psychotherapy that are taken for granted and sound so easy but are exceedingly difficult. (p. 26)

A phenomenological emphasis, then, is one that stresses the significance of relating to another by *felt* communication, by an experienced interchange, rather than by observation or by an evaluative approach. From this viewpoint, human exchanges are understood and dynamically known rather than verbally described. The term "existential" in the psychological sense leads to the same emphasis in interpersonal relationships but originates from a distinction between "essence" and "existence." In philosophy this problem is a crucial one and has involved innumerable disputes and academic problems throughout the centuries.

In current philosophical debates, Sartre's extreme nihilistic philosophy has brought this problem to the forefront again. Sartre claims that existence in man precedes his essence and as a result man *is* his choices. This is a philosophical problem and must first be solved on an ontological basis. In psychology, the existential emphasis has quite a different significance because it is primarily concerned with "existential" as meaning the reality of this individual person as he "exists," here and now, in his anguish, in his emotional distress, rather than in this or that categorization. The existential psychological approach concentrates on the "existence" of this suffering person as preceding the "essence" of his pathological syndrome. In other words, this emotionally distressed person is more important than his symptoms; and the psychologist aims to help the person instead of concentrating on his deficiencies. In this derived sense, the psychological differentiation has very little to do with the ontological problem of precedence in regard to essence and existence. As Rollo May (1961) says, "Existential means centering upon the *existing* person; it is the emphasis on the human being as he is *emerging, becoming*" (p. 16). He clarifies this position further: "In psychology and psychiatry the term demarcates an *attitude*, an approach to human beings, rather than a special school or group" (p. 18). Consequently, the range of thought and beliefs within this emphasis is extensive, including Hassidic theologians such as Buber, atheistic writers such as Sartre, and Christian thinkers such as Marcel.

In using *phenomenological* in its more generic sense, then, we emphasize (but do not overlook the importance of other aspects) the knowledge and understanding of the human person in his existential reality. The phenomenological approach to personality endeavors to transcend man's behavior, defined in terms of traits and characteristics, and to comprehend him as he exists dynamically in his pulsating, emerging, becoming, and living self. He is this person in his uniqueness, as contrasted to this member of the group, this percentile on the graph, this number on the list.

The historical development of philosophical phenomenology and existentialism is complex, and current theories require a profound study to attain even the fundamentals. In psychology and psychiatry, the influences of these theories continue to grow because they offer deeper insight into the dynamic functions of the individual.

> A century ago, in his profound analyses of anxiety, Kierkegaard offered us a tremendously acute and prescient insight into the problem which philosophers, theologians, and many psychoanalysts see as characteristic of man's experience in our own time. Kierkegaard helps us understand the loss of self-hood, the problem of estrangement (self-alienation), utter loneliness, and the nature of anxiety. (Ruitenbeek, 1962, p. xiii)

CONTEMPORARY PHILOSOPHY

Contemporary philosophers are interested in the propositions of the existential writers from the standpoint of ontology.

Psychologists and counselors are more interested in these writers' descriptive analyses of dynamic functions of modern man in
his conflict with himself and his being-in-the-world. Existential
philosophers have made astute psychological observations.
Many of these psychological concepts are scattered throughout
the works of Kierkegaard, Jaspers, Marcel, Heidegger, Sartre,
and others. Since no one of these philosophers attempted to
present a complete psychological explanation of the human person, there is no "existential" theory of psychology in the strict
sense of the word. But a true interest in the psychology of the
human person will naturally seek beneficial elucidations of the
existential person, i.e., of the person as he lives, thinks, experiences, and feels in his immediate everyday existence.

For example, one of the most pervasive mental conflicts of
contemporary man is his struggle with anxiety. Many circumstances and scientific discoveries have created conflicts for modern man that did not afflict his predecessors. Today, technology,
nuclear warfare, and discoveries in outer space have tightened
the tensions of dread and loneliness that each human being carries within himself. These new threats of sudden and complete
destruction bring man much closer to his confrontation with
death. For many, death and destruction are more proximate
and threatening than they have been for other generations, and
the problems of anxiety, consciously or unconsciously, are more
intense and more widespread. In the search for a more penetrating knowledge of anxiety, psychologists have found many
helpful and illuminating passages in *The Concept of Dread* written
by the Danish philosopher Kierkegaard (1941). Complete and
profound studies of dread and anxiety are scarce and Kierkegaard's description is one of the most vivid.

Influenced by Kierkegaard and others who describe the
emerging conflicts of man, modern philosophers have included
valuable psychological insights in their philosophical pursuits.
Husserl's interpretations of subjectivity have evoked a considerable number of research studies in this direction. Influenced by
the "reality of subjectivity," the counselor becomes more aware
of the person in his thinking and feeling self as well as in his behaving self. True, all are interwoven, but what we grasp first is
what we see before us, and this is the man in his outward behav-

ior. Behind the outward man lies the profundity of his conscious and unconscious feelings and cognizing self. Until we come to know something of this interior domain we have only skimmed the surface.

Husserl

Husserl is the philosopher who chronologically follows Kierkegaard and precedes the contemporary existential writers. For our purpose he forms a link between philosophical phenomenology and existentialism. Husserl developed a concept of human reality in terms of dynamic intention which differs distinctly from the traditional philosophical notion of substance. Husserl himself rigorously adhered to a philosophical exposition of his principles and was not concerned with man's inner experiences. Husserl's philosophy differs from that of existentialists, particularly in regard to the concepts of existence and essence. Husserl adhered to an emphasis on essence in contrast to some of the existentialists who give precedence to existence. But his intentional theory and method of descriptive analysis have given a definite direction to philosophical movements. It is the shift from a rational, abstract emphasis to an experiential, concrete interpretation that is so beneficial for psychological studies.

For a psychology of human personality, Husserl's influences are indirect, since he did not draw examples from human behavior as many of his successors did. He sometimes seemed to resent applied examples drawn from his philosophical principles. However, what is important for the study of personality and counseling is the awareness of an intentionality described by Husserl. By "intentional" is meant the internal dynamic sources that give rise to individual behavior.

Nevertheless, it is difficult to find an adequate explanation of personal identity in the philosophy of Husserl. Perhaps this will be a problem that modern philosophers will untangle in the course of time. Personality defined as man in his relatedness is truly a dynamic process, ever changing, moving in realms of concrete reality, linking the person with the world in which he lives and with which he communicates. But this individual is more than his relatedness. He retains within himself a cer-

tain permanent selfhood, the core of his identity, and continues to exist as *this being* despite his psychological and physical
variabilities.

Heidegger

Heidegger introduced the concept of *Dasein*, a German
word to describe man as being-in-the-world. The problem of
Dasein is an ontological one and relates to man's existence in a
world of space and time with consequences of finitude and responsibility. But from a psychological viewpoint, this emphasis
on man's "being-in-the-world" forms the crux of his personality.
This description puts man in his true psychological context, because a man lives always in a world of otherness, and his lifelong
pursuit hinges on his ability to cope with his social existence. He
must endure and surmount the inevitable conficts arising from
his destiny as this being in a world of otherness.

The counselor must know a person in this precise condition
and not as an isolated figure. A reflex theory is inadequate, particularly in this challenge to comprehend man's subjective experiences as they arise in his meeting and struggle with himself and
with his world. This complexity of man as a being-in-the-world
with all that it implies reaches beyond his physiological systems.

This is the task that confronts the counselor as he endeavors
to be of help to the disoriented client. He must help the distressed person communicate with others, for every person who
suffers anguish is somehow faced with certain barriers sepa-
rating him from the "world" in which he finds himself. He is
not at home in his situation. When he can exist effectively as a
"being-in-the-world" his tensions diminish and his creativity and
productivity increase.

Jaspers

Jaspers has endeavored to clarify the position and value of
philosophy and science, and has insisted that both disciplines are
necessary to comprehend man's existence. He has skillfully described the uselessness of a system of philosophy or a view of

man that stresses either to the exclusion of the other. He deplores the failure of either reductionism or idealism alone to offer valid explanations of man's ontological existence. These clarifications of science and philosophy and the need for both form a more complete background for a true psychology of personality. They help to unfold the unified nature composed of both subjective and objective realities. Within man these two domains are joined and give a particular quality of "humanness." A psychological theory that ignores either explanation is lopsided, and gives a distorted view.

Jaspers holds that within man these two aspects of existence are joined by his freedom of choice. Jasper's description of choice differs fundamentally from the Sartrian notion of freedom; the latter is identified with man's essence. But for Jaspers, man is free to choose even in the face of an Absolute Being. For Sartre, man is *condemned* to choose, because there is no absolute outside of himself. While these two positions are philosophically poles apart, the emphasis on man's inner freedom and the importance of decisions and choices in his whole life cycle are significant for personality studies. Jaspers indicates often that "being-oneself" must meet the inevitable conflicts of "being-there," i.e., of living in a world of reality, and that in doing so man continues his process of existence. Man in his personal existence engages in conflicts, experiences guilt, suffers, and inevitably meets death. What Jaspers (1960a) brings home forcibly for the counselor is the need of studying man in his entirety, in his personal existence and relationships. To ignore or minimize either is to falsify the human situation.

> The truth is that man is accessible to himself in two ways: as object of inquiry, and as existence endowed with a freedom that is inaccessible to inquiry. In the one case man is conceived as object, in the other as the non-object which man is and of which he becomes aware when he achieves authentic awareness of himself. We cannot exhaust man's being in knowledge of him, we can experience it only in the primal source of our thought and action. Man is fundamentally more than he can know about himself. (p. 63)

Marcel

Gabriel Marcel refers to the irreducible nature of being as a mystery, not unknowable, but rather a real experience, not completely explicable. This position is maintained through many descriptions of love, freedom, encounter, and other concepts. For example, Marcel reminds us of the various analyses that explain the nature of love, although love eludes description in actual experience.

Marcel (1961) often refers to "presence" as a qualitative reality of meaningful human relationships. Presence is also an experience, irreducible to complete objective analysis. "Presence is mystery in the exact measure in which it is presence" (Marcel, 1961, p. 36). For many of his philosophical descriptions, Marcel offers examples drawn from psychological experiences. "Presence is something which reveals itself immediately and unmistakably in a look, a smile, an intonation or a handshake" (p. 40).

Playwright as well as philosopher, Marcel (1961) has created characters who demonstrate ontological principles as they occur in life. It is precisely this emphasis on human relationships that enhances our understanding of personality. All human relationships revolve on love, and insofar as a human person is capable of loving, so is he capable of relating positively to another. Handicapped by psychological deficiencies, a human person will be limited in his power to love and to extend himself to others. These are psychological facts. Marcel's notion of presence, its indefinable nature, and the power of its reality deepens our understanding of interpersonal relaionships.

Intersubjectivity is another concept which Marcel (1961) uses to describe human exchanges based on love. By this term Marcel demonstrates the decisive difference between two persons related on a subject-to-subject basis and things related to one another because they occupy space, side by side. "When I put the table *beside* the chair I do not make any difference to the table or the chair, and I can take one or the other away without making any difference; but my relationship *with* you makes a difference to both of us and so does any interruption of the relationship make a difference" (Marcel, 1960, p. 222). Marcel's discourse on intersubjectivity illuminates nuances, real in the existential but not in the objective sense. All of these fine points constitute the warp and woof of human exchange and consequently, of personality and counseling. They are directly related to basic problems of personal integration and social adjustment.

Marcel's doctrine of participation insists on the inseparability of the subject from that in which it participates. By this notion he tries to explain the interior quality of all human experiences ranging from the simplest feeling to the most sublime form of contemplation. The counselor must give more consideration to these existential discernments. They show human beings in movement, in the flux of becoming, and not merely as outward spectators disjointed from their own behavior. "It seems to me now that the spectator, in the ordinary sense of the word, makes as if to participate without really participating; he has emotions which are superficially similar to those of people who really are committed to some course of action or other, but he knows very well that in his case such emotions have no practical outcome" (Marcel, 1961, p. 151).

Marcel's comment is psychologically very meaningful. To know a human person in his deepest reality is to know him in his commitments. Knowing another, being of help to another, requires an understanding of this person in his various participations, i.e., in relation to himself and to all others with whom he is concerned. Personality springs from within, is formed and shaped by attitudes, ideas, and the whole range of inner dynamics. Superficial appraisals of the personality imply that the person is a "spectator" surrounded by aggregations of traits, mathematical formulas, or percentile norms. These are far removed from the existential experiences they aim to represent and, at best, tell us something about the outer shell that may even hide the inner self.

Sartre

Sartre's nihilism and contradictions expose a certain absurdity in his position, and show by the radical nature of that position the great need for a positive philosophy of man. Psychologically, Sartre's philosophy of despair, hate, condemned freedom, and nothingness offers little more than a state of "non-being" akin to that of the acutely depressed psychotic. However, from another standpoint, Sartre's influences cannot be overlooked. In his philosophical and literary works he has included strikingly intuitive and revealing psychological insights. Certain descriptive details of human feelings and behavior are more illuminating for the counselor than the basic theme of nihilism and "condemned" freedom with their contradictory principles. Sartre severs human relationships, at least in theory, and reduces them to absurdity. In doing so he vividly portrays a sick personality. The human person, totally separated from all others, nothing in himself, condemned to choose his own fatality, and culpable for his inevitable sins against himself cannot survive long in a state of positive selfhood, nor can he know effective exchanges with others. There is a certain tyranny in Sartre's extravagant nihilism and if we follow him literally there should be nothing more welcome than death. But this is not usually the case of the person who is glad to be alive. Sartre's philosophy presents the human person as a very loosely knit assembly of activities with little chance for uniqueness, identity or individuality.

> There is no reality except in action . . . Man is nothing else than his plan; he exists only to the extent that he fulfills himself; he is therefore nothing else than the ensemble of his acts, nothing else than his life . . . What we mean is that a man is nothing else than a series of undertakings, that he is the sum, the organization, the ensemble of the relationships which make up these undertakings. (Sartre, 1957, p. 32–33)

Sartre puts the person on a shaky foundation. When we identify man with his actions we still give no adequate accounting for the sources of his activities. Sartre gives no basis for individual identity, no essence for its reality. Though an individual's personality changes, as a human being he is more than the ephemeral "ensemble" which Sartre describes.

Apart from his philosophical discourses, Sartre offers some interesting descriptions of choice. His examples give a realistic glimpse into our responsibility for our choices. Contrary to the deterministic implications of his nihilism, they describe the meaningful changes in each person's yielding and choosing.

> What people would like is that a coward or a hero be born that way . . . What the existentialist says is that the coward makes himself cowardly, that the hero makes himself *heroic*. There's always a possibility for the coward not to be cowardly any more than for the hero to stop being *heroic*. What counts is total involvement: some one particular action or set of circumstances is not a total involvement. (p. 34–35)

Sartre injects a surrealistic quality into the nature of perceptual images and reveals his unusual sensitivity to sensory experiences. His knack for vivifying sensory qualities suggests the possibility of other perceptual dimensions. "The *true* sea is cold and black, full of animals; it crawls under this thin green film made to deceive human beings" (Sartre, 1959, p. 167). For the counselor, Sartre's descriptions are more valuable than his principles since the latter are contradictory and seem to cancel each other. But his portrayal of subjective processes is graphic and suggests new facets of the inner dynamic world.

Buber

The works of Martin Buber, including treatises on theology, philosophy, and the psychology of man, are among the most valuable contributions to contemporary personality theory. The mystic nuances and poetic style of Buber's writings distinguish them from other current works but do not obscure the depth and validity of his intuitions. Buber's concepts of man's subjectivity and his profound grasp of man's inner relationship with himself and others have opened new vistas of thought. Buber's I-Thou relationship is the cornerstone of his philosophy of man and offers enlightened revelations of man's essential relationships with others. In many aspects Buber's theological and psychological interpretations are in contraposition to those of Sartre's atheistic expositions. Both, however, offer an existential emphasis.

Sartre's interpretations of the human person are finally based on a negative doctrine, and human relationships turn out to be mostly ones of hate and aversion. On the contrary, Buber's interpretation of the human person is basically one of self-realization. He speaks of the individual moving toward an absolute, enriched in this forward movement, by commitments to other human beings, engagements of unselfish love. The essentials for a true, dynamic, and creative theory of personality will be found in Buber's basic concepts. It remains for us to understand their application. While Sartre's insights bear some significance for the abnormal, disintegrated personality, Buber's approach is oriented toward man in his fullness and in his synthetic wholeness. His works help us to discern the human personality in its positive fulfillment and in its mature becoming. For this reason they are more valuable appraisals of the human personality in its normal and positive development. Buber's (1958) belief that "All real living is meeting" (p. 11), summarzies his thought. For the psychologist, Buber's insights offer new dimensions for a theory of personality. In his further discussions and in the sequel to this exposition of his primary doctrine, *Between Man and Man* (1955) Buber includes his ideas of directness, present-ness, mutuality, all of which relate essentially to the formation of personality. He describes the differences between an "I-It" relationship, man's awareness of himself as different from what he perceives; and the "I-Thou" relationship, a reciprocal, meaningful relationship between two human beings. In the first relationship man perceives an outside world outside, but in the second, his whole self is engaged with the existence of another human being. In this process his own becoming increases as he relates to the Thou with his whole being.

All of these valuable distinctions reveal the intricate movements involved within ourselves and in our relationships with others. In these discussions Buber has contributed more directly to the study of personality than have other contemporary philosophers. He has penetrated more intuitively into the inner beingness of man and his social nature. With Buber's help we can understand the need to experience these exchanges in order to develop normally. His philosophy of mutuality integrates values and unifies man's relatedness within himself, to others, and to his being-in-the-world.

> If you consider the individual by himself then you see of
> man just as much as you see of the moon; only man with
> man provides a full image . . . Consider man with man, and
> you see human life, dynamic, twofold, the giver and the re-
> ceiver, he who does and he who endures, the attacking
> force and the defending force, the nature which investi-
> gates and the nature which supplies information, the
> request begged and granted and always both together,
> completing one another in mutual contribution together
> showing forth man. (Buber, 1955, p. 205)

Mounier

One of the most brilliant and stirring interpretations of man
as a person in his dynamic living has been written by Mounier.
The works of Mounier bristle with criticisms against mechanistic
pressures arising from false religious emphases that reduce man
to a robot. Cut short by an untimely death, Mounier's personalism is incomplete but remains an influential testimony to man's
individuality. In describing man in his fullness of being and living, Mounier (1952), opposing depersonalizing concepts, tries to
revive the dignity and significance of each person.

> Since the person is not an object that can be separated and
> inspected, but is a center of re-orientation of the objective
> universe, we shall now have to turn our analysis upon the
> universe that it reveals in order to elucidate its structures
> upon different levels. Of these we must never forget that
> they are only different angles of vision of the same reality
> . . . (p. xxxiii).

For an understanding of the human personality in its
wholesomeness and beneficial becoming, we must consider the
person as the center of the material world that surrounds him
and not as an object, or thing useful in industrial production. In
order to be himself and to fulfill himself by relating and living
with others, the human person must have freedom from duress,
from the push and pull of mechanical forces, and also from religious concepts tinged with predestination or fatalism.

Another important aspect developed by Mounier is that of personalism as opposed to extreme individualism. Mounier describes the stifling effects of a smug attitude that builds up the self by indifference to others. A person cannot be truly himself without relating to others, ". . . the truth of each depends upon its relation to the others" (Mounier, 1952, p. xxviii). No matter how talented or gifted this individual may be, his essential worth can only be realized in meaningful communication with others. Although some of his descriptions become too segmented, we find in Mounier's philosophy certain basic principles for the understanding of human personality.

Mounier carefully distinguishes between man, as the center of a material universe, superior to it because of his human dignity, and *this* man, as "de-centered" from himself so as to be open to others. In the latter sense, Mounier opposes the excesses of individualism that overlook man's essential need for others.

With a spirit of openness to others the human person communicates more freely. And Mounier further distinguishes the need for mutual communication as opposed to mass communication or collectivity, which may counteract the very foundation of a real person-to-person exchange.

In summary, Mounier's philosophy places the human person in the center of his material universe and endows him with personal dignity and rights derived from his intrinsic worth. "Thus, if the first condition of individualism is the centralization of the individual himself, the first condition of personalism is his decentralization, in order to set him in the open perspectives of personal life" (Mounier, 1952, p. 19).

Later in the same discussion Mounier concludes, "Thus the positive interpersonal relation is a reciprocal provocation, a mutual fertilization. . . . Personalism, therefore, refuses to attach a pejorative coefficient to social existence or to its collective structures" (Mounier, 1952, p. 24, 27).

Mounier also emphasizes a "decentered" maturity in each individual that enables him to grow and increase in his mutuality with others. Rejecting determinism, collectivism, and extreme individualism, he stresses man's worth, his social nature and personal significance.

Ricoeur

More directly related to Husserl than to contemporary existentialists, Paul Ricoeur has contributed significant insights into man's dynamic movements. Ricoeur maintains that man has two basic commitments arising from the duality of his spiritual and animal nature. Because of the opposite movements which this dual essence embraces, an inevitable struggle results. Torn between these two powerful tendencies within himself, man's existence is involved in a constant strife immersing him in anguish. Ricoeur maintains that this human conflict is an ontological factor and not only a warfare against evil. This distinction between the ontological and mortal in regard to man's existence, nature, and inevitable anguish is one of the most illuminating contributions to modern thought. For pastoral counselors especially, this particular clarification brings order into explanations formerly vague or relegated to the moral or spiritual order. Many confusions in modern research have arisen from semantics which neglected to differentiate between moral and psychological factors. This precise explanation of man's conflict as ontologically based, helps to resolve the differences between certain psychological problems that cause anguish, and moral failures that cause remorse. True, all are interwoven and interdependent within each human being, but a realistic comprehension of man in his existential living must take account of these differences.

Ricoeur's emphasis on the significant intentional distinction between voluntary and involuntary activities brings into focus certain aspects that likewise bear meaning for human behavior and interest the psychologist. This emphasis is directed toward the object in the case of involuntary movements and toward the subject in the case of voluntary movements. The two are not entirely separated but are distinguished according to their sources and their intentional relationships. For example, the object of hunger is involuntary. A person who experiences hunger is aware of a condition within himself that arises whether he desires it or not. What he does about this object, fulfilling it or evading it, is an action he performs voluntarily. The pangs of hunger, then, are involuntary objects of hunger; they arise from involuntary sources. The actual hunger is different from my awareness of it, and, in one sense of the word, becomes the object of my awareness. The voluntary movement differs intentionally from the involuntary experience. It is more intimately within the person as subject, and the person himself performs, acts, and chooses an object exterior to his own action (not necessarily exterior to his person). These are intentional distinctions, i.e., subjective differentiations that explain behavioral changes and value modifications.

The intentionality of our emotional and feeling experiences distinguishes the object from the emotion or feeling. For example, when we say this person is lovable, this task is difficult, this insect is detestable, the lovableness, or difficulty, etc., is not in the object, but in the person who experiences it. This is an important distinction for the counselor. Another individual may have opposite experiences with the same "objects." He may not experience love toward this same person, or a difficulty in this task, or an aversion for this insect. All of these experiences of emotions and feelings may be caused by objects; but the specific feeling or emotion itself is a subjective, intentional experience of the person who has the emotion. These considerations help us to clarify the nature and sources of our dynamic processes. However, these experiences of realizing lovableness, difficulty, etc., are not autonomous, but depend on the objects with which this person relates. It is the object perceived, known, and felt that forms the basis of reality and the basis of substantial objectivity.

> The hateful and the lovable are "meant" on things but do not have the peculiar subsistence of objects the observation of which one can never complete. They are only qualities which must be "founded" on the perceived and known objects in order to appear in the world. The nature of these intentional correlates is such that they cannot be separated from the representative moments of the thing; they are intentional correlates but without autonomy. It is the perceived and known object which endows them with a center of significance, a pole of objectivity and, one might say, the substantive of reality . . . (Ricoeur, p. 127–128).

Personality from a phenomenological point of view is the human person in his relatedness. As a person, he retains oneness and identity, but his personality continues and *becomes*, as he relates to others, to situations, and to objects of all kinds. We cannot separate the personality from the person, but we can and must distinguish these concepts. This distinction is real, subjective in origin but anchored in the objectivity of things outside of the experiencing person. Ricoeur's explanation of intentionality in this particular area helps us to grasp more clearly this subtle but vital point. He further explains that the reciprocal action but modal difference between feeling and knowing demonstrates the separation of object and subject. The subject (this person) is "detached" objectively from something he knows and about which he may have some feeling. Thus, in order to know, he must know "something." Related to objectivity, both knowing and feeling share an intentional nature, though they differ in mode. A feeling for an object indicates a direction of movement toward or away from it, while knowing an object does not. To know an object is to possess it internally, but to have a feeling for it is an additional experience.

> Here the reciprocity of feeling and knowing is very illuminating. Knowing, because it exteriorizes and poses its object in being, sets up a fundamental cleavage between the object and the subject. It "detaches" the object or "opposes it" to the I. In short, knowing constitutes the duality of subject and object. Feeling is understood, by contrast, as the manifestation of a relation to the world which constantly restores our complicity with it, our inherence and belonging in it, something more profound than all polarity and duality. (p. 129)

These are just a few examples from some of the outstanding phenomenological and existential writers of recent times that help us to penetrate more profoundly the inner sources of the human person. Certain others such as Blondel, Max Scheler, Berdyaev, Unamuno, Tillich, Ortega y Gasset, Merleau-Ponty, and Medard Boss have written scholarly treatises that help us to fathom man's complexity. Each one has concentrated on certain specialities that enhance our understanding. A thorough study of each of these writers is helpful; but for our purpose we can quote only a few in order to indicate the new sources available to psychologists as well as philosophers.

REFERENCES

Allport, G. (1955). *Becoming*. New Haven: Yale University Press.

Basescu, S. Human nature and psychotherapy: An existential view. *Review of Existential Psychology and Psychiatry*, Vol. III, No. 2, Spring, 1962.

Buber, M. (1958). *I and Thou*. New York: Charles Scribner's Sons.

Buber, M. (1955). *Between man and man*. Boston: The Beacon Press.

Heidegger, M. (1949). *Exixtence and being*. Chicago: Henry Regnery Co., Gateway Edition.

Jaspers, K. (1960). *Way to wisdom*. New Haven: Yale University Press.

Kierkegaard, S. *Fear and trembling* and *The sickness unto death*. N.Y., Doubleday, (trans, 1941).

Kretschmer, E. (1926). *Physique and character*. New York: Harcourt Brace.

Lindner, R. (1956). "Songs my mother taught me," *The fifty-minute hour*. New York: A Bantam Book, 1956.

Marcel, G. (1960). *The mystery of being*: (Vol I) Reflection and mystery. Chicago: Henry Regnery Co., Gateway Edition.

Marcel, G. (1961). *The philosophy of existentialism*. New York: The Citadel Press.

May, R. (1961). *Existential psychology*. N.Y.: Random House.

Mounier, E. (1952). *Personalism*. Notre Dame: University of Notre Dame Press.

Ricoeur, P. (1967). *Fallible man, Part II, Finitude and guilt*. Chicago: Henry Regnery Company.

Ruitenbeek, H. (1962). Some aspects of the encounter of psychoanalysis and existential philosophy in *Psychoanalysis and existential philosophy*. New York: E.P. Dutton and Co., Inc.

Sartre, J.P. (1957). *Existentialism and human emotions*. New York: The Philosophical Library.

Sartre, J.P. (1959). Nausea. New York: A New Directions Paperbook.

Sheldon, W.H. (1954). *Atlas of men: A guide for somatotyping the adult male at all ages*. New York: Harper & Row Publishers.

Tillich, P. (1952). *The courage to be*. New Haven: Yale University Press.

INDEX